MW00831223

Ruins and Resilience

Sonics Series

Atau Tanaka, editor

Sonic Agency: Sound and Emergent Forms of Resistance, Brandon LaBelle

Meta Gesture Music: Embodied Interaction, New Instruments and Sonic Experience, Various Artists (CD and online)

Inflamed Invisible: Collected Writings on Art and Sound, 1976–2018, David Toop

Teklife / Ghettoville / Eski: The Sonic Ecologies of Black Music in the Early 21st Century, Dhanveer Singh Brar

Dissonant Waves: Ernst Schoen and Experimental Sound in the 20th Century, Sam Dolbear and Esther Leslie

New for 2024

Take This Hammer: Work, Song, Crisis, Paul Rekret

The England No One Cares About: Lyrics from Suburbia, George Musgrave

Building a Voice: Sound, Surface, Skin, Zeynep Bulut

Goldsmiths Press's Sonics series considers sounds as media and as material – as physical phenomenon, social vector, or source of musical affect. The series maps the diversity of thinking across the sonic landscape, from sound studies to musical performance, from sound art to the sociology of music, from historical soundscapes to digital musicology. Its publications encompass books and extensions to traditional formats that might include audio, digital, online and interactive formats. We seek to publish leading figures as well as emerging voices, by commission or by proposal.

Ruins and Resilience

The Longevity of Experimental Film

Karel Doing

Goldsmiths
Press

Copyright © 2024 Goldsmiths Press
First published in 2024 by Goldsmiths Press
Goldsmiths, University of London, New Cross
London SE14 6NW

Printed and bound by Short Run Press Limited, UK
Distribution by the MIT Press
Cambridge, Massachusetts, USA and London, England

Text copyright © 2024 Karel Doing

The right of Karel Doing to be identified as the author of this work has been asserted by him
in accordance with sections 77 and 78 in the Copyright, Designs and Patents Act 1988.

Every effort has been made to trace copyright holders and to obtain their permission for the
use of copyright material. The publisher apologises for any errors or omissions and would
be grateful if notified of any corrections that should be incorporated in future reprints or
editions of this book.

All Rights Reserved. No part of this publication may be reproduced, distributed or
transmitted in any form or by any means whatsoever without prior written permission of
the publisher, except in the case of brief quotations in critical articles and review and certain
non-commercial uses permitted by copyright law.

A CIP record for this book is available from the British Library

ISBN 978-1-915983-02-2 (hbk)
ISBN 978-1-915983-01-5 (ebk)

www.gold.ac.uk/goldsmiths-press

Goldsmiths
UNIVERSITY OF LONDON

Contents

Acknowledgements

First and foremost, I am indebted to all the artists, filmmakers and collectives mentioned in this book. My individual achievements only make sense within a broader context. Parts of this book are autobiographical, and I have taken the liberty to write about my own work. However, my aim is to go beyond my individual point of view and contribute to a broader understanding and appreciation of experimental cinema as an art form.

In the ensuing chapters, besides the numerous films and performances mentioned, there are many references to the written word. It has been particularly enlightening to find articles and statements by fellow filmmakers, complemented by interviews undertaken by critics and scholars. These texts have provided me with guidance and inspiration to develop my own perspective on 'practice-based research'.

In addition to the sources referenced throughout this book, many other remarkable publications have appeared in the past few years that have had a profound impact on my thinking and writing, such as *Experimental Filmmaking: Break the Machine* (Ramey, 2015), *Process Cinema: Handmade Film in the Digital Age* (MacKenzie & Marchessault, 2019), and *Experimental and Expanded Animation* (Smith & Hamlyn, 2018). I am honoured to make a small contribution to this growing field of research.

Without the series editor, Atau Tanaka, this book would not exist. Only through his enthusiasm and support have I gained the necessary confidence to gather my scattered ideas, finish half-written essays, and assemble everything together into one (hopefully) coherent whole. I also want to mention Angela Thompson and Ellen Parnavelas, who guided me through the editorial and production process, and the reviewers, who provided me with sharp-witted critical notes that have been extremely helpful.

Furthermore, I want to express my gratitude to professor William Raban, Dr Kim Knowles, Liz McQuiston, Dr Milena Michalski, Dr Elio Della Noce, and Chris Dymond for stimulating conversations, for giving me the opportunity to publish, for helping me to improve my writing skills, and much more.

During some of the most difficult moments of the writing process, my wife, Ekaterina Yonova-Doing, supported and challenged me. Without her I would be lost. Our daughter, Violeta Valentina, is my greatest inspiration; she not only stands for the future but has also helped me to sharpen my thinking about cinema, perception, and consciousness, simply by being there.

List of Illustrations

Introduction

As an experimental filmmaker, I started from pure practice. My first films were based on simple ideas, and I worked in a generative way. I didn't even see myself as an experimental filmmaker – I was finding ways to express myself, and film happened to be a medium that worked for me. Together with two fellow artists, Saskia Fransen and Djana Mileta, I founded a Super 8 film laboratory in 1989 (Studio één). To build this organisation from scratch, I had to communicate in writing with many people and institutions. This wasn't too hard as I had outspoken ideas about art and society. I also had to write synopses to promote my films. This was more difficult: my practice was guided by my hands, eyes, and ears and was not informed by words. I often wrote just a few descriptive sentences, focusing on methods rather than concepts. Meanwhile, my network grew fast, and I met many artists and filmmakers who worked in a similar way, not bothered by script writing, film theory, or history. We agreed that work should be made, seen, and experienced, instead of being theorised and historicised. When we exchanged information, it was mostly practical: how to do X, how to find material Y, how to operate machine Z. A thriving community evolved based on this hands-on, practical-minded, and improvisatory approach.

However, as our audience grew too, it became more diverse and more demanding. Why did we still work with photochemical film? What does this particular image sequence mean? What is the relation between famous filmmaker X and your work? Often, I did not have clear answers to these types of questions. Intuitively, I knew, but putting this 'knowing' into words was not an easy task. Almost twenty-five years after the founding of Studio één, I moved to London and quickly became part of a much more theory-oriented circle of artists and filmmakers. This was refreshing and inspiring, and I started thinking about doing a practice-based PhD project. In a series of conversations with veteran filmmaker and educator William Raban, my ideas started to take shape. The University of the Arts London accepted my proposal, and for the next four years, I plunged into reading, debating, and writing. It was a challenge to write about 'pure practice', reapproaching this way of working from a theoretical and historical perspective. My thesis turned out to be just the beginning of a much longer journey. This book is an accumulation of work done over a period of ten years and includes the inquiry of my doctoral thesis, albeit in a much further-developed form.

Chapter 1 explores the 1980s Super 8 scene and its links to punk, no wave, and industrial music. Chapter 2 unpacks the importance of do-it-yourself (DIY) culture and the beginnings of the current artist-run labs network. Chapter 3 examines the reappropriation of abandoned spaces and alternative depictions of the urban fabric. Chapter 4 discusses alchemy as an influential method within experimental filmmaking. In chapter 5, the neat division between old and new media is questioned via an investigation of the creative use of archival footage and the reintroduction of redundant technology. Chapter 6 discusses the global expansion of the artist-run labs network with examples from Latvia, Indonesia, and Mexico. Additionally, the appearance of disaster, collapse, disappearance, and malfunction within contemporary experimental films is discussed. Chapter 7 looks at film grain, noise, and the emergence of meaning. Chapter 8 investigates co-creation as a form of direct action. Chapter 9 focuses on the impact of posthumanism and new materialism. Chapter 10 subsequently explores the importance of postcolonial thinking. In the final chapter, these different strands are brought together in a discussion of my work with plants, chemistry, and film. Some of these chapters partially overlap with previously published texts. Chapters 3 and 4 include citations taken from interviews with expanded cinema artists conducted during my doctoral research (Doing, 2017). Chapter 8 is a shortened version of my article 'Cinema and the Prefigurative' published in *Culture Unbound* (Doing, 2023). Chapter 9 partially overlaps with my chapter 'Experimental Film Practice and the Biosphere' that will be included in the *Palgrave Handbook of Experimental Cinema* (Doing, 2024). And in chapters 10 and 11, I am reformulating some of the ideas that appear in 'Phytograms: Rebuilding Human-Plant Affiliations' (Doing, 2020) and 'Les Réalités Désordonnées du Cinéma Multispécifique' (Doing, 2022). While the aforementioned texts are primarily focused on eco-criticism and co-creation, this book has provided me with an opportunity to explore gender, the postcolonial, and the Global South in more depth (in chapters 5, 6, 9, and 10).

My overall aim is to say something useful about experimental film while walking a fine line between the practical and the theoretical. The difference between my approach and a purely academic one is that I find myself in the middle of the action. To my mind, this is an advantage, not a disadvantage. But of course my insider perspective does shape my point of view. I am not objective. Being aware of this, I have unapologetically mixed autobiographical elements and descriptive passages with analytical views and philosophical musings, confirming my insider perspective rather than hiding it. I have used my own work as a guideline for structuring the book. This has given me the opportunity to focus on a multifaceted journey through experimental film practice while also providing an overarching narrative. The book starts in the 1980s, a moment in time that is usually connected with the decline of experimental film, not with a rebirth. You won't find much about films and filmmakers of earlier periods in here. This is a book about a (poorly documented) recent past, a thriving present, and an uncertain future. Instead of being informed by a belief in linear progress, my perspective is inspired by curiosity. Experimental film is like an exploration – the fact that you do not know what exactly lies ahead of you is appealing. An analogy can be made with wandering through an unknown land: 'The horizon carries the promise of something more, something *other*' (Abram, 1997: 210). According to Abram, the horizon stands not only for a yet-undisclosed future but also for a receding past. He concludes that 'these dimensions are no more temporal than they are spatial, no more mental than they are bodily and sensorial' (ibid., 215). This can be transposed perfectly to experimental film practice. Film is a time-based medium, a strip that travels through a projector in a straight line from head to tail. And yet, the experience of making and watching experimental film stretches out in multiple temporal, spatial, and physical directions.

This brings me to another important point: the fact that I not only love making experimental films but I also love watching them. Finding myself in the role of the spectator seemed entirely obvious when I started participating in festivals and other events. I enjoy watching films without the need for a narrative or a conclusion. But this experience is precisely what needs further unpacking. What exactly is this inexplicable experience? What does it mean to abandon narrative and embrace the phenomenological? In my film descriptions and analyses, I have attempted to focus on an open form of spectatorship, starting from the experience itself, not from a theoretical departure point. The theory comes after, not before. For me the, crux of the matter is what I see, hear, and sense when I watch a film. That might sound very unsurprising, but in many analytical accounts this is not the case. Theory is put first, and the real experience is explained away, to be ruled over by historical frameworks, a neat ordering of concepts, and a eulogising of the greats. My own analysis is more messy, deliberately so. I want to ask myself again and again what exactly touched me. This results in a winding path, as I allow myself to go forward, backward, and walk in circles. There is no ultimate destination but a rich set of forks, tunnels, and vistas that can be encountered along the way.

I already noted that I have used my own work as a structuring principle for this book. In almost every chapter, you will find a discussion of one or more of my films and performances. For me, making new work always coincides with an engagement with the work of fellow artists and filmmakers. In each chapter, I have done this by examining the works that were on my radar at that particular moment in time. The films described and analysed are picked because they address a particular idea, concept, or experience. In many cases, these are films that have gained widespread recognition, but lesser-known works also appear. Nowhere do I intend to eulogise my own work and compare my achievement with the works of others. Instead, I hope that by uncovering my own practical and theoretical insights in relation to those offered by the work of others, I will help the reader gain a deeper understanding and a broader appreciation of contemporary experimental film. The filmography at the back of the book lists the URLs of the films that are publicly available. Fortunately, many experimental filmmakers are extremely generous with their work and make their films available online. Of course, nothing compares to an actual screening, but with the links provided, the reader will be able to see and experience in a home-cinema setting some of the works discussed.

The starting point of my book might appear as an awkward moment to the well-informed reader: since the 1980s, the film industry has gone through an unprecedented period of downsizing. Service providers and manufacturing companies have either disappeared completely or have successfully entered the market for digital media. The production of many film stocks has ceased, and the remaining products have become more expensive. It is also more difficult to purchase these products: companies focus on big industry buyers and give little attention to artist-run labs and individuals working with film. This grim situation notwithstanding, the contemporary experimental film community has not only found ways to survive but is actually thriving. With their communal DIY approach, they have safeguarded a future for their own medium. Equipment has been salvaged and repaired, an international network has been established, knowledge has been made accessible through online databases, a free exchange of information has become the norm, independent archives are taking shape, and alternative solutions to formerly industrially produced equipment, services, and materials are being developed as we speak. In parallel, the countercultural dreams that were central to experimental film culture in the '60s and '70s have changed shape. The zeitgeist of the 1980s was very much defined by a negative outlook on the future. Unfortunately, today's world is indeed still plagued by inequality, war, and dictatorial regimes. Even in democratic and socially liberal countries such as the UK, where I live, inequality grows, racism hasn't disappeared, gender equality still needs to be fought for, weapons trading flourishes, international cooperation stalls, and democratic values wane. These social ills have certainly not disappeared from the agenda of contemporary experimental filmmakers, but such issues are addressed without the overambitious zeal of the countercultural movement. Instead, a new form of activism has emerged, for the present-day community utopia is not a far-flung island but a hard-won interval in the here and now. This type of practical resistance appears recurrently in this book, particularly in chapter 8.

Besides practical innovations and political context, this book also looks at topics such as trance, alchemy, and cosmology. These themes are not new and can be found in the work of artists and filmmakers throughout the history of art in general and experimental film in particular. While narrative fiction and nonfiction films mostly address such subject matter indirectly by telling stories *about* mystery, cosmos, and transcendence, experimental filmmakers look for ways to turn the cinematic event *itself* into something otherworldly by exploiting the inherent qualities of the medium. The prolific film historian Tom Gunning provides a precise analysis of the importance of the hidden mechanisms and their effects which make motion picture film such a powerful medium:

The primary purpose for creating optical illusions may not lie in simple deception, their ability to fool someone into taking them for 'reality'. Rather, such illusions operate to confound habitual attitudes toward perception, indeed sowing doubts about the nature of reality. These doubts could play a pedagogic role in either rational systems (teaching that perceptual systems are not to be trusted, but must be buttressed by knowledge of scientific causes and the demonstration that the scientific method calls for) or transcendent systems of belief (teaching that mere perception is fallible; only faith in transcendence can make sense of creation). (Gunning, 2004: 30)

Such an oscillation between rational and transcendent systems is pertinent in the context of contemporary experimental film practice. What is remarkable in recent approaches is that artists are not choosing either the rational *or* the transcendental but instead are seeking a *coincidence* of both points of view. The material, chemical, and optical nature of film is a particularly suitable playground for experimenting with such an approach which is partially steeped in science while being equally open to metaphysics. This aptitude comes up throughout the book, most prominently in chapters 4 and 7.

Working with photochemical film is an activity that involves the whole body. Equipment is weighty, emulsion is fragile, water flows abundantly, fumes are hazardous, meticulous handiwork is required, patience is tested, brains are racked. In comparison, digital filmmaking hardware and software are designed to be light, fast, convenient, and clean. Experimental filmmakers deliberately choose their messy, slow, and demanding medium. The gain is that the photochemical film practice offers a more holistic experience that connects the somatic with the cognitive. Also, the immanence of photochemical film in the world is much more tangible in comparison to the presumed 'immateriality' of digital media. Although this contrast between material and immaterial can be easily refuted, the important point is that film is both reliant on and responsive to the natural world and our bodies: the silver halides of photographic emulsion are embedded in gelatine (an animal product); the reductive processes in a darkroom mimic similar processes in nature; mixing chemicals is very close to cooking dinner; the surface of a filmstrip resembles a skin that can be touched or wounded; and a shutter in a camera or projector reminds us of our own fluttering eyelids. These themes – body, embodiment, environment, immanence, and entanglement – are discussed in the final part of this book.

The diversity of subjects and approaches does not make it easy to condense the focus of this book into one paragraph. However, two major ideas stand out: redundancy/innovation and touching with the eyes. In spite of the widely declared redundancy of photochemical film, the experimental film community has been on the path of innovation. This is a major theme that I explore in multiple ways: by looking at the roots and flourishing of the artist-run labs network, by formulating a contemporary theoretical framework, and by highlighting the individual achievements of filmmakers who have made work that surprises, confronts, educates, and resonates in new ways. The second theme, touching with the eyes, is equally omnipresent. Accentuating the material qualities of film has long been a strategy in experimental film, but it has been reshaped from being primarily engaged with analysis/reflexivity into an inquiry of the perceptual/environmental. In projection performance, expanded cinema, and other alternative forms of presentation, a similar shift can be seen. To question our own perception implies the existence of other forms of awareness. It is no longer just the illusion produced by the machine that is under scrutiny but also our own senses and our place in the world among other species. When our eyes can touch, responsiveness is boundless. Seeing is proof of reality, touching is intimacy with the real. Contemporary experimental film, then, is a practice that constantly renews itself, a practice that seeks an intimacy with the world, a world brimming with light, sound, and life.

1

Savage Cinema

In 1986, I shot my first reel of Super 8 film, animating a series of woodblock prints picturing the sun. I instantly fell in love with the medium and explored its possibilities further, combining moving images with sculpture, performance, drawing, and painting. The next year, I made an installation based on a dialogue between my body and my workspace. That workspace was in flux as I was living and working in squatted buildings in Arnhem and Nijmegen, in the eastern part of the Netherlands. My idea was to swap body for building and vice versa, using my physique as a structural element and the architecture as a living, and breathing entity. At that time, it was relatively easy to occupy abandoned buildings without being evicted immediately, hence the success of the squatting movement. Artists and activists found each other, crafting a pragmatic alliance that made it possible for the movement to gain the necessary traction. Not everybody shared the ideology of the more politically oriented members, and not everybody shared the romanticism of the creatives, but each faction tolerated the other. Before joining the squatting movement, I had considered pursuing further education in a technical direction, but in the end I decided to go to art school, enthused by my parents, who had a high regard of the arts and had always encouraged me to make things. In parallel with this combined technical/artistic interest, I was trying to make sense of my own fluid gender. I had a strong urge to explore my tender masculinity as my father had been hiding his feelings altogether. My concept allowed me to explore these underlying themes, using my naked body as a mathematical vector in space and an abandoned factory as a spirited life form in an installation titled *Fort/Vlees* (1987). I filmed a series of movements on Super 8 black-and-white film, exploring the three-dimensional space provided by film frame and lens. These movements were in turn derived from a wooden structure found and photographed in a squatted building that was in the process of being renovated and legalised (see figure 1.1). The films were projected on small screens made of ground glass that I had incorporated into a slender but angular sculptural object that included positive/negative woodcuts, echoing its initial conception. This interest in the body and

Figure 1.1 Study for film installation *Fort/Vlees* – Karel Doing (NL 1987, bw photograph).

architecture coincided with themes that were also explored by one of my favourite music groups, Einstürzende Neubauten. I had bought their 1981 release *Kollaps* fascinated by their raw and passionate sounds and by the photo on the back showing the band with a collection of instruments/ tools in front of the Olympiastadion in Berlin. The thumping, grinding, and screeching noises that are accompanied by the talking/singing/screaming of lead singer Blixa Bargeld resonated with my own unruly attitude. In her authoritative study of the group, Jennifer Shryane highlights the concept of 'architecture as a performance' as one of their key ideas (Shryane, 2011: 16). During their initial years, the group regularly performed on urban sites, exploiting unusual acoustics and foraging pieces of scrap metal to be used as percussion instruments. The role of architecture in their work reaches further, as exemplified by the already-mentioned album cover displaying the group as renegade workers/ musicians that would certainly qualify for the label *entartete kunst* (degenerate art) in front of the stadium that was used by the Nazi Party as a propaganda tool in 1936. And of course it is reflected in the name of the band itself, which exposes the shaky foundations of the hastily built and ideologically informed new architecture that had sprung up on both sides of the divide after the Second World War.

However, my practice was not at all based on theoretical musings and can be better described as a form of pure practice or 'savage cinema'. I had never even heard of experimental film and its further subgenres like structural film or visual music. In my next Super 8 work, I used my naked body again, albeit in a more psychodramatic way, painting a nest of snakes crawling over my torso (*Vlaag*, 1988). I am thinking of this sequence now as a kind of magical incantation to ward off the depressing rhetoric of the Cold War with its language of mutually assured annihilation. The work was born out of a need to articulate the terrifying prospect of nuclear war and to express the darkness and despair that came with the possibility of an apocalypse caused by human 'ingenuity' (see figure 1.2). Much later, I found out that the two approaches, the first being more formal and the second being more dramatic and personal, placed me with one foot in structural/materialist filmmaking and with the other in what might be called expressionist filmmaking. I will return to this marriage across the divide several times in this book, demonstrating how this conjoining of styles and ideas has refreshed and innovated experimental film practice.

Figure 1.2 *Vlaag* – Karel Doing (NL 1988, Super 8 film, bw, 1min).

One of the highlights of the visual arts course that I was following was a series of lectures by practitioners. Amongst the invited artists was Babeth Vanloo, a Dutch underground filmmaker who had worked with the Sex Pistols, Joseph Beuys, Lydia Lunch, and many other artists. She was teaching at the Vrije Academie (Free Academy) in The Hague and facilitated a 16mm shoot for me and Saskia Fransen, my partner and fellow artist, using an Arriflex camera in their well-equipped studio. The resulting two-minute film (*Hondekoppen*, 1990) features an angry squatter's rant, a barking dog, and a pile of plates being smashed to bits. My education in what would be generally called 'underground film' gathered speed soon after I graduated from art school. Together with Saskia and a third art student and Super 8 enthusiast, Djana Mileta, I had set-up Studio één, an artist-run laboratory. We had acquired professional film printers that allowed us to make Super 8 contact prints and blowups to 16mm. Through this initiative, I got in touch with many artists and filmmakers who were working in Super 8, amongst them the riotous film academy student Ian Kerkhof (now Aryan Kaganof). Kerkhof organised a series of public screenings, inviting radical filmmakers from a variety of backgrounds. One of the screenings that particularly impressed me was dedicated to the New York–based Richard Kern. His early Super 8 work includes two intense collaborations with singer, poet, and actress Lydia Lunch. Both artists are associated with the Cinema of Transgression movement. Kern impressed me with his virtuoso handling of the Super 8 camera, while Lunch opened my eyes with her provocative statements about sexuality and power relations. The Cinema of Transgression had already passed its heyday, reaching notoriety with films, performances, and writings that deliberately provoked everybody that could be provoked. Interestingly, Nick Zedd, the leader of the pack, published a manifesto in which he ranted against a previous generation of artists/filmmakers still largely unknown to me at the time:

We who have violated the laws, commands and duties of the avant-garde; i.e. to bore, tranquillize and obfuscate through a fluke process dictated by practical convenience stand guilty as charged. We openly renounce and reject the entrenched academic snobbery which erected a monument to laziness known as structuralism and proceeded to lock out those filmmakers who possessed the vision to see through this charade. (Zedd, 1985)

The importance of this statement is that it signifies a fissure between two generations of experimental filmmakers. In Zedd's eyes, structural filmmaking did represent the establishment, hence his fierce attack on a form of filmmaking that has been widely eulogised as a radical critique on mainstream cinema. Instead of a careful dismantling of the cinematic apparatus, as practiced by structural filmmakers, the alleged members of the Cinema of Transgression simply smashed things to pieces, seeking to hurt the audience by punching them in the gut with images of vomiting, violence, and suffering. But beyond this aggressive attitude, there was room for more sophisticated ideas as well. In his informative study *Deathtripping*, Jack Sargeant proposes a form of positive nihilism or 'Dionysian affirmation' (Sargeant, 1995: 28) as a conceptual underpinning. Sargeant defines 'transgression' as a creative action rather than a destructive one:

Transgression gives the simultaneous experience of both radical disruption and a reformulation of limits. It neither fully breaks or returns the limits that we perceive, instead it continually works to define those limits, a process that allows us to see how our present limits (which are never totally static), are constructed. (Ibid., 36)

The best-known image coming out of the Cinema of Transgression can be found on the cover of Sonic Youth's album *Evol* (1986). This image is taken directly from Richard Kern's film *Submit to Me*, released in the same year. The film starts with a strip-and-bondage sequence filmed from a camera angle that looks down; the characters are filmed crawling and rolling on the floor. Harshly lit and drenched in red, black, and purple, the erotic feel of the opening shot is immediately distorted. The action is set in a gritty New York apartment covered in graffiti and black paint. Not much is revealed other than mattresses on the floor and sparse furniture. Lydia Lunch's appearance in the first shot seems to fit loosely in a heteronormative universe, but this approach is shattered in the following shots featuring androgynous characters performing increasingly deviant actions. When Lunch returns, she transforms her miniskirt into a penis and jerks off, provocatively looking at the camera. When the letters 'D E S T R O Y' appear, the action gets more violent and disturbing. A woman in bondage struggles and screams. Her protest appears to be disturbingly realistic and is addressed at the camera, implicating the spectators in the abusive situation. Next, the camera creeps up on Lung Leg, the young woman featured on the cover of Sonic Youth's *Evol*. Her eyes are wild, she scratches at the camera, and smears a dark lipstick on and around her lips. The next scene is straight out of the Wiener Aktionismus (Viennese Actionism) playbook, showing a naked couple covered in what looks like blood. This short sequence is followed by a series of shots of a woman in a ballgown who seemingly produces a stiletto from her vagina, wildly stabbing at the camera/spectator. The next confrontation depicts a young drug addict injecting and overdosing, his body going limp and his face changing into a death mask. The film reaches a further climax with a series of bloody stranglings and executions and ends with a series of closeups of a man covered in blood screaming in agony before he lets go and finally relaxes his body.

Submit to Me can be easily dismissed as hollow, perverse, or misogynist, but to my mind the film deserves a second look. In a move reminiscent of structural film, *Submit to Me* attempts to make the viewer aware of the fact that the cinematic apparatus is a system that is inherently hierarchical. By breaking the fourth wall, the film implicates the viewers in the act of looking – in this particular case, not an innocent way of looking but a highly voyeuristic one. Additionally, gender roles are muddled, either playfully or radically. Domination and submission go both ways, as do aggression and ultimately murder. The film is both misogynist and misandrist, celebrating the destruction of the body in all directions. But this destruction is reversed by presenting acts of sexual aggression in an ecstatic way: death − climax = sex. Not only do the actors submit them-selves to the camera, allowing the spectator to lust after their bodies, but simultaneously the spectator is force-fed with a triangulation between the attractive, the repulsive, and the nihilistic, which leaves them breathless and exhausted after viewing the film. This sheds more light on Sargeant's characterisation of the movement as a form of 'Dionysian affirmation'. *Submit to Me* is a negation of the 1960s antiwar slogan 'Make love not war'. But this certainly does not mean that the film mindlessly promotes sexual aggression. Rather, the film reminds us of our inherent sexuality and bes-tiality. However, in the interview included in *Deathtripping*, Kern largely avoids a more analytical way of questioning his films and simply states that 'the best part of anything is watching' (Sargeant, 1995: 102). Contrarily, his collaborator Lydia Lunch is much more explicit about her motivation: 'And with truth as my basic tenet, these films are going to insult and assault a lot of people because it is not entertainment I'm after, it's reality I'm deal-ing with. The ugliest of realities at that' (Davis, 1995: 178). Besides their collaboration in *Submit to Me*, Kern and Lunch have co-written two more films: *The Right Side of my Brain* (1985) and *Fingered* (1986). Both films are disturbing narratives about abuse, with Lunch starring as the sexually insane girl who not only allows men to abuse her but passes on her abuse to anybody weaker than her. She elaborates further in the interview: 'All you know or feel is pain because that is what you have been taught. All you know is how to distribute and inflict pain on yourself and others. My films are a way of trying to understand the whole psychology behind that process' (ibid., 180). Her presence on the set of *Submit to Me* might have been more than merely acting in Kern's voyeuristic fantasy but also push-ing his limits, forcing him to transgress the boundary between fun and truth telling.

An equivalent to this exploration of sexuality and power relation-ships can be found in the experimental Super 8 films made by the prolific director Derek Jarman. I discovered Jarman through the New Romantic Film Movement, a British group of filmmakers who mainly worked on

Super 8. Several members of the group took part in an exhibition at the Amsterdam-based art gallery Aorta with a Super 8 film installation. The spacious gallery was in one of the famous squats in Amsterdam, the former *Handelsblad* newspaper press. In the Netherlands, squats were a breeding ground for alternative art, and several artist-run organisations (*kunstenaarsinitiatief*) were established during the early '80s, such as W139, de Fabriek, and Oceaan. These exhibition places had a lasting impact on the regional development of the arts (see further Vriens, 2016). The Super 8 film installation in Aorta was made in the typical style of the New Romantic Film Movement. The critic and programmer Michael O'Pray provides a concise summary of their approach:

New Romanticism was a cinema of what, at the time, seemed untrammelled excess: using rich colour, superimposition, continually moving camera and an elaborately theatrical *mise en scene*, which mixed high-art iconography and popular culture, and more controversially, sado-masochistic gay imagery culled from cinema, performance art, fashion and photography. (O'Pray, 2009: 343)

Jarman was an important figure in the New Romantics movement and both inspired the associated filmmakers and borrowed ideas from their work in return. His films *The Angelic Conversation* (1984) and *The Last of England* (1987) were shot on Super 8 and are much less conventional in their storytelling than his historical dramas such as *Caravaggio* (1986). *The Angelic Conversation* is a bittersweet and melancholic film that weaves together shots of eroticised young boys with ominous images of burning cars and a radar installation. A poignant image shows a young man intently staring at a skull. The duration of the film obliges the spectators to surrender to the excessive use of grainy slow-motion imagery which is soaked in yellow, green, and sepia hues. The sound is equally atmospheric, with dark ambient music composed by the experimental music group Coil interspersed with the voice of Judi Dench reading a selection of Shakespeare's sonnets written to an unnamed young man. Her voice is drenched in reverb pushing the already-longing tone of the poetry into a realm that evokes forlorn gothic architecture. In *The Last of England*, this burning desire turns into something much more destructive, bringing the work closer to films such as Kern's *Submit to Me*. The film opens with a sequence in which Jarman himself appears, writing in a voluminous diary. These images are intercut with a scene in which an intoxicated young male tramples and beats a Caravaggio painting. His aggressive behaviour changes into a sexually charged performance when he crawls on top of the thrashed painting. The next sequence uses visual alliteration, drawing associations between the lighting of a cigarette, the young man walking in circles with a boat flare in his hand, and shots of workers welding and hammering. Subsequently, images of the young male who prepares to inject himself lying among the rubble are intercut with home movie shots of British family life procured from footage shot by the director's father. Shaky images of demolished and blackened industrial buildings are accompanied by a crowd chanting 'England England England'. Servicemen dressed in boiler suits and balaclavas aim their automatic rifles through the shattered windows of a building. The film mixes artistic performance with documentary footage, fictionalised actions, and home movies, blurring the line between the real and the imagined. Characters and locations keep reappearing, suggesting a narrative in need of completion by the spectator. The film makes use of a variety of editing techniques freely gleaned from both mainstream and experimental cinema, for example, in a fast-paced sequence that brings together silhouettes of industrial buildings photographed at dawn, uniformed men with automatic rifles, naked contorting bodies covered in blood, and costumed men who perform a kind of ritual. The crumbling landscape of the Docklands plays a prominent role in the film, dominating the aimless protagonists with a grotesque redundancy. The importance of this location is commented on in the anthology *Taking Place*:

The Royal Victoria Docks provide a place where histories collide. Both a site of contemporary political struggle in the rise of right-wing neoliberalism in Britain and a relic of the industrial past, the abandoned docks and quays, with their curious decrepit beauty in the midst of late modernity, provide a place of historical rupture. (Turner, 2009: 94)

A third (unnamed) movement, with similar attitudes, emerged within the walled-off confines of West Berlin. This amputated city became a refuge for young Germans escaping compulsory military service. The district Kreuzberg with its dilapidated housing stock sprang back to life energised by the radical squatting movement, and became a cultural platform for a marginalised generation of artists, musicians, and filmmakers. Squatted homes were in dire need of maintenance, while band recordings, film productions, and art exhibitions were realised on shoestring budgets. This growing DIY culture embraced Super 8 film and cassette tapes, media that were both relatively cheap and widely available. Artists often combined an interest in music and film, which resulted in all kinds of crossover projects that involved film projection, live and/or taped music, and performance. One of the most prolific artist of this scene was undoubtedly Michael Brynntrup, who spearheaded a monumental collective film that was shot on Super 8 black-and-white film. Cartridges of cheap Soviet film were smuggled back and forth across the border, bringing artists from the East and the West together in a highly symbolic sharing of technology and creative goals. The resulting two-hour-long *Jesus – The Film* (1981) can be described as a Dadaist recounting of the life and suffering of the prophet. The film comprises thirty-five episodes made by twenty-two contributors, with Brynntrup being the constant presence as leading protagonist and organiser. After touring extensively with the film in Europe and North America, the artist started working on a new series of short films, brought together under the name *The Ivory Elephant,* a cycle of 'dance macabres' or death dances. The loyal agent in this case is a skull that appears in each episode. A number of different characters all relate to this skull in their particular way. The characters are queer, criss-crossing boundaries between male and female, abled and disabled, self and other. Death is brought upon them by disease, war, self-destruction, and black magic. But ultimately, the series reflects a reconciliation with death, celebrating its all-conquering and equalising power. Nuclear war turns into a liberating experience, deformity into beauty, and the skull into a unifying means to reflect one's own mortality.

My own introduction to Brynntrup's work took place during the AVE festival, an event with an international focus organised by tutors and students affiliated with the art school in Arnhem where I was studying. The penultimate episode in the series, *Die Botschaft – Totentanz 8* (1989), starts with an image of a heap of decaying leaves mysteriously bursting into flames and smoke. A monumental staircase appears, dramatically lit by light flooding through broken windows. The camera zooms in on the silhouette of a woman in evening dress. She stops at a birdcage that she encounters on the landing, lifting the cage carefully while reaching inside. In a theatrical manner, she throws the down feathers from the cage into the air while climbing the stairs, thus creating specks of light that descend slowly, disappearing into the darkness of the staircase. The film cuts to a series of images of a ruinous space; negative images are juxtaposed with positive images. The woman enters this space in a flare of solarisation, positive and negative image alternating rapidly. She dances more wildly, swinging the cage back and forth. Her repetitive motions are enhanced and eroticised by means of flickering re-photography, slow motion, and the use of extreme closeups. The sequence ends when she exits the frame, after which the film cuts to black. A static image of a skull resting on a window sill appears against a backdrop of neoclassical architecture. The image alternates between black-and-white and colour, and the skull is replaced by the heap featured in the opening shot. The woman enters and reclines on the window sill, letting a handful of feathers blow away with the wind. Carefully, she picks up the skull, brings it to her lips, and explores the empty cavity with her tongue (see figure 1.3). The inter-title 'ENDEND' interrupts the film, after which the heap returns, with sparks shooting out from hidden fireworks. A second inter-title proclaims 'ENDE' and is followed by a solarised image of the female protagonist joyfully throwing feather down.

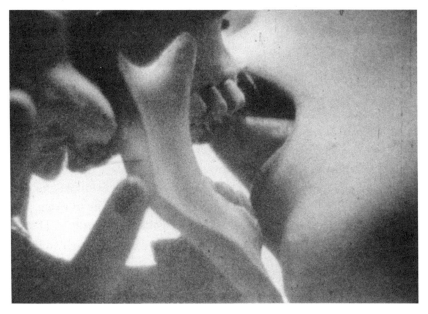

Figure 1.3 *Die Botschaft – Totentanz 8* – Michael Brynntrup (DE 1989 Super 8 film, bw, 10min); courtesy of the artist.

Die Botschaft – Totentanz 8 represents just a tiny element of Brynntrup's oeuvre, but the film does include several elements that can be found in other films by this productive filmmaker. The final scene, in which the woman embraces death, takes on an additional meaning if one reads Brynntrup's biography, published on his website: 'Identical twin brother stillborn. Since then studies in Philosophy. The artist lives and works' (Brynntrup, 1959–∞). The skull therefore represents not only the death of the other but also the death of the twin brother, or more broadly, the death contained within one's self. Brynntrup often uses self-portrayal in an ironic way, investigating his own mortal body and imperfect consciousness. Also, the play with language, exemplified by the inter-titles 'ENDEND' and 'ENDE' is typical across his work. Both themes are explored extensively in later films such as *Die Statik der Eselsbrücken* (1990). Brynntrup's work has been looked at in the context of New Queer Cinema (Kuzniar, 2022), but his characters (including his self-portrayal) represent gender identities in a state of flux. This instability opens up Brynntrup's films to different types of film spectatorship beyond the dominant male gaze but not confined to a 'gay gaze' either. His language games demonstrate the fluidity of the meaning of words: through deliberate small shifts in spelling and by means of editing an inter-title that normally signifies the end of a movie, words/letters/language suddenly take on a number of possible meanings. A similar relational game is being played with the spectator, whatever their gender identity is. Such an unstableness can also be found in the previously described film *Submit to Me* by Richard Kern. Of course Kern leans much closer to a typical male gaze, but his S/M inclination drastically undermines a mainstream sugar-coated version of heterosexual love. In contrast to the ironic, sophisticated, and humourist practices of Brynntrup, his New York colleague Kern rips open an old wound and pokes around wildly in order to disturb and hurt the spectator as much as possible, while simultaneously exposing himself to that same audience in the worst possible way. Laura U. Marks's investigation into S/M spectatorship is relevant in this context:

> To recognize the contingency of power on position makes it possible to enjoy the privileges of power in a limited way. This includes the privilege of temporal alignment with a controlling, dominating, and objectifying look, with being a spectatorial 'top'. It also includes the pleasure of giving up to the other's control, experiencing oneself as an object, being a 'bottom'. (Marks, 2002: 77)

This openness to different gazes is what makes *Submit to Me* unpalatable to many members of the audience who prefer to hide their more extreme fantasies and desires from public view. Similarly, Jarman's *The Last of England* caused a scandal as it effectively portrays England as a society replete with S/M relationships. The young protagonist we meet in the opening scene is simultaneously gay and macho, underdog and dominator. All of this is exposed within a few minutes through Jarman's use of a visual language that brings together a collection of symbols taken from different cultural and political identities: a sculpted male torso, military boots, an abandoned warehouse, grainy black-and-white film, and a renaissance painting. This set of symbols is brought together by means of a well-articulated voice-over written by an erudite man. The queerness and perversity of this combination was not well received by everybody, apparently touching a sore spot. Historian Norman Stone's often-quoted qualification of the film as depicting 'sick scenes from English Life' (see, for example, Monk, 2014: 8) is brilliantly reversed in *Private Practice, Public Life*:

The Last of England thus suffers under a political sickness, inscribed on the body of England, on its architecture and landscape, and more directly, onto the bodies of those excluded (from health, from home, from jobs) under a regime that would make (private) patients of us all. But it is also a beautiful film: Jarman suggests that sickness need not be shackled to images and terms of weakness and stigma, but may empower a different register of social and artistic health. (Lippard & Johnson, 1993: 286)

To me as a young filmmaker, the work of Jarman, Kern, and Brynntrup was inspiring and formative as it did show me possible approaches relevant to my practice – a practice that was concerned with identity, the body, anxiety, aggression, and sexuality, alongside more formal and aesthetic concerns. A less often discussed element of these experimental Super 8 films from the 1980s is their focus on architecture as a site of performance. As already mentioned above, the industrial ruins of the Docklands take on a prominent role in Jarman's *The Last of England* not only as a tangible synecdoche of Thatcherite politics but also as the director's personal habitat: 'Jarman lived on the river Thames in disused warehouses in varying states of decline, and it was in these abandoned buildings that he developed fully his artistic and filmmaking practice' (Turner, 2009: 79). Political reality and personal history are seamlessly conjoined in Jarman's collage.

The decaying industrial landscape acts both as a metaphor for national malady and as a depressing document of an all-too-real situation. The same coincidence between urban reality and creative use of space can be seen in Brynntrup's *Die Botschaft – Totentanz 8*. Kreuzberg and other parts of Berlin were full of decaying buildings that were every so often re-appropriated by a young generation of artists and activist. In the film, this common reality is represented in a complex way. The opening scene with the staircase is strongly reminiscent of 1920s German expressionist film, such as *Das Cabinet des Dr. Caligari* (1920), but the exposition of the upstairs space uses formalist elements related to structural filmmaking as a way to denote a transitory phase between life and death. This short sequence is followed by the longer solarised dancing sequence that uses this photochemical effect as a further exploration of negative and positive space. The swirling effect of this technique, which is difficult to control, suggests an amalgamation of two separate realities. Finally, the row of columns that are framed by the glassless window can be understood as a theatrical space that is more tolerant of the magical and the transcendental. In my other example, *Submit to Me*, the architectural space is also important, albeit much less visible. Many shots are filmed against an altogether white or black background, similar to an infinity white space and a black box that can easily be created in a professional studio. But when we look more closely, it is apparent that the film was not shot in a studio at all but in an almost empty run-down New York apartment. The words 'EVOL' and 'DEATH' are graffitied in a corner, the dirty floorboards show no sign of homeliness, the walls are smudged and cracked, and much of the apartment is shrouded in an ink-black darkness. This setting underpins the nihilistic and transgressive aims of the filmmaker. Architecture, then, is not merely a location with objective parameters but functions as an actant in the associative web that each of the discussed Super 8 films weaves. The dilapidated state of the architecture in these films is no coincidence but reflects the era of the Cold War and severe economic depression. The answer of a young generation of filmmakers was to take things in their own hands and creatively use the spaces that they re-appropriated in their quest to find a new form of expression.

More broadly, these examples show how a new generation of experimental filmmakers broke away from the formalist concerns of structural/

materialist filmmaking while simultaneously still being concerned with the problematic relationship between spectator and moving image. Instead of an austere aesthetic and a focus on empty spaces and screens – signature elements of the previous generation – the new experimental films were filled with naked bodies, expressive colours, thick shadows, and theatrical elements. But these young filmmakers also borrowed ideas and techniques from their predecessors. The graininess of Super 8 film was embraced and sometimes enhanced, and structuralist (in-camera) editing schemes were embedded in often discontinuous narratives. This approach to film-making can also be seen in the work of Helga Fanderl, Marcelle Thirache, Schmelzdahin, and Luther Price, all filmmakers and groups who started working on Super 8 film in the 1980s. The structural/materialist approach that had dominated the previous decade remained influential, but the sometimes-dogmatic approach practiced by filmmakers in the late 1970s was replaced by a more hybrid form of experimentation, freely combining punk, industrial, queer, and formalist methods. In my own early experiments with Super 8 film, I experimented with my body and gender identity, along with exploring real and cinematic space and time. My practice was spontaneous and intuitive: I did not have much historical knowledge or theoretical insight. However, my own work and the work of many of the above-mentioned filmmakers was informed by a DIY ethos. The films referenced in this chapter, including my own, were made on rock-bottom budgets. Making something with nothing was characteristic of this time, a time defined by the Cold War, youth unemployment, and economic slumps. The next chapter will look at this DIY approach in more detail.

2

DIY

This chapter discusses the beginning of the artist-run labs network, a community that finds its roots in the 1980s squatting movement. Squatting is an activity that requires ingenuity and resolve. Upon entering an abandoned building with a patchy roof, deliberately stripped of electricity, water, and heating, new occupants had to improvise in order to make their quarters liveable. Out of necessity, many creative solutions were found, and a wave of small-scale artistic, cultural, and social activities materialised. No Future turned into do-it-yourself (DIY). The philosophy of this movement is succinctly captured by artist and activist John Jordan: 'If the problem is one of values – a cultural problem – it therefore requires a cultural response' (Jordan, 1998: 130) This cultural response is characterised by an urge to do things and a focus on self-empowerment rather than discussion and debate. DIY happens in the here and now, unencumbered by history or theory. Besides the limitations that such an approach might have, it generates energy and creative resolve, overcoming malaise and complacency. DIY seeks to act and create with immediacy, in an improvised and generative way. Improvisor David Toop highlights the importance of such an approach:

Humans must learn to improvise, to cope with random events, failure, chaos, disaster and accident in order to survive. Yet as an antithesis to this improvisational necessity, we find an insidious culture of management strategy, militaristic thought, planning and structured goals expanding through all social institutions, a desperate grasping at simplistic political antidotes to global and economic instability. In this context, the central role of improvisation in human behaviour is consistently devalued. (Toop, 2016: 1)

DIY (as a formative methodology within the squatting movement) was an international affair, and the movement not only was successful in urban centres such as Amsterdam and Berlin but also flourished in many smaller cities around Europe. In 1983, a group of artists and activists occupied a former cardboard factory in Grenoble. The re-appropriated factory, now affectionately renamed Le 102, is situated in the Berriat district, a neighbourhood that used to be the centre of industrial activities. The squatters transformed the building into living quarters, studios, and an event space: hosting concerts, performances, and film screenings. This first successful transformation was followed by a wave of squatting, remodelling the quarter into a centre of cultural and creative activity. Public activities were not only aimed at insiders but also designed to involve the broader community. The success of this movement subsequently convinced the local authorities to tolerate the squatters and, in some cases, such as the collective Brise-Glace, support their activities. This artist-driven regeneration attracted further individuals and enterprises working in the creative industries (see further Michel & Ambrosino, 2019). Le 102 is still continuing their activities at the time of writing, demonstrating the robustness of the original movement.

A young experimental photographer, Christophe Auger, who was involved in the programming of the event space, also worked in a professional photo lab, a job that provided him with detailed knowledge about lesser-known photochemical processes such as black-and-white reversal and E6 colour development. He used his technical skills to develop his own photographs, slides, and Super 8 films. In 1987, he was joined by Xavier Quérel and Jerome Noetinger to form the projection performance group Cellule d'Intervention Metamkine. Quérel had good knowledge of electrical engineering and used his skills to repurpose 16mm projectors, making the machines more versatile within a live performance setting. The third member of the group, Jerome Noetinger, is an improviser, composer of electro-acoustic music, and publisher, bringing with him an extensive network. Under these favourable conditions, Metamkine (their shortened name) toured extensively around France and the rest of Europe, often performing at music festivals while also gaining attention within the experimental film scene. In 1993, the group took part in the Audio Visueel Experimenteel (AVE) Festival in Arnhem and visited Studio één, the Super 8 lab established by me, Saskia Fransen and Djana Mileta a few years earlier in Casa de Pauw, a large squatted complex that had been successfully legalised. The lab was based in former stables, in the back of the large garden surrounding the complex (see figure 2.1). Studio één aimed to provide facilities for artists and filmmakers who worked independently with no or very little funding. The main idea was to pool resources, an approach that was common within the squatting movement. Therefore, the principal aim of the foundation was to make the lab accessible to kindred spirits. With the financial support of my father, the foundation acquired professional laboratory equipment, a Super 8 contact printer, and a Super 8 to 16mm optical printer. These machines came from a commercial lab that had been catering to well-to-do amateurs and was now switching to video. After receiving an additional small grant from a local fund, the foundation obtained further second-hand equipment such as a Super 8 editing table and multiple cameras. As mentioned in the previous chapter, Super 8 technology was rapidly becoming obsolete, and the prices of second-hand equipment were falling, while the film stock was still widely available, making the medium more popular with artists.

After their visit to the lab in Arnhem, Auger and Quérel decided to follow Studio één's open-door policy. At what became known as MTK

Figure 2.1 Studio één (NL 1990); photograph by Karel Doing.

(a further shortened version of the name of the performance group), fellow artists could hand-process Super 8 and 16mm film and use a JK optical printer to manipulate their footage. In the following years, a lively exchange of information ensued between Studio één and MTK about film stocks, developing methods, equipment, and screening opportunities. My own technical knowledge was patchy as I had no formal technical training. I had mostly picked up information by reading books such as Lenny Lipton's *Independent Filmmaking* (1972) and by talking to professional lab technicians. The exchange with MTK was very welcome and enriching. Meanwhile, their performance in Arnhem was part of a series of events that also included an expanded cinema performance by the German filmmaker Jürgen Reble. The festival organisers had asked me to assist him during a workshop dedicated to hand-processing. Reble first demonstrated the black-and-white reversal process, working with Super 8 film and Russian-made developing tanks. After teaching this straightforward technique that produces realistic images, he quickly moved to the next step, altering the image with a range of tinting and toning techniques, solarisation, and more destructive measures such as attacking the film with permanganate bleach. (His alchemic approach to filmmaking will be discussed in more detail in chapter 4.) Equipped with much more knowledge about processing and printing, we expanded the activities of Studio één further.

A similar expansion took place in Grenoble. Filmmakers such as Gaëlle Rouard, Etienne Caire, and Olivier Fouchard were able to develop their work in MTK, not only using the resources but also actively contributing to the growing knowledge base that the lab represented. The absence of a formal or hierarchical structure led to an explosion of creativity but also put increasing pressure on the core members of the collective. In 1995, a meeting was organised to announce that MTK would become private again but continue to offer guidance in support of new artist-run film labs. Soon several new labs were established, such as Mire in Nantes, l'Abominable in Paris, and Burstscratch in Strasbourg. The situation in the Netherlands was equally lively. Together with Saskia Fransen, I organised a series of open screenings that took place in the living space above the studio. By doing this, we were able to connect with some of the key figures who were working on Super 8 and 16mm at the time. The programme was screened at the local arthouse in Arnhem and in two alternative venues that were linked to the squatting community, Filmhuis Cavia in Amsterdam and 2B in Eindhoven. Two years later, we initiated a collective film project, *Vitaal Filmen* (1993), an omnibus film consisting of eleven sections, each representing a part of the body – some quite literally focusing on the anatomy of the body, others taking on the subject in a metaphorical way. The film was distributed in a hybrid network of squats, arthouse theatres, and festivals, exceeding the first programme in reach. Meanwhile, another artist-run organisation dedicated to analog film was established under the name Filmstad. This organisation was focused on providing 16mm postproduction and had no interest in setting up laboratory facilities. A highly successful series of monthly screenings was organised, showing new work by members and guests alongside a curated selection of short films. Individual artists and groups from other countries took part in this lively exchange of ideas as well, and the initial informal exchange between Studio één and MTK grew into a well-organised international network encompassing labs in France, Belgium, Germany, and the Netherlands. Between 1995 and 1999, the labs published a collective zine under the name *l'Ebouillanté* (Filmlabs, 2022). In a dedicated issue of the long-running *Millennium Film Journal* titled 'Fundamentals' the experimental filmmaker, producer, and gallerist Pip Chodorov summarised the significance of this movement:

Now it was a hands-on process from start to end, in which a multitude of personal choices led to a new look: a non-standard color scheme, a chosen level of abstraction or surrealism, graininess or roughness. One could modify the chemical recipes, the times or the temperatures, or skip processes. On the optical printer, shots could be slowed down or accelerated, zoomed in, flipped around. On the contact printer one could play with exposure, superimposition, loops, negative imagery, reprinting many generations, color separation, or any new technique we could invent. (Chodorov, 2014: 30)

A recurring proposition in online articles and journals about the new artist-run labs was that the London Filmmakers' Cooperative (LFMC) functioned as a model for the newly established labs (see, for example, Catanese & Parikka, 2018). This proposition is only partially true, as the people at both MTK and at Studio één (including myself) had very limited knowledge of the history and founding principles of the LFMC. Instead of being 'based on' it, what happened was more a reinvention of the concept that was very much informed by the specific situation at hand. As already mentioned, both Studio één and MTK were established in squatted buildings and rooted in DIY culture. George Mckay's validation of the DIY movement provides some further insight:

Housing and homelessness, the environment, unemployment, the social value of people, the construction of community, poverty, cultural entropy and silence – all of these, and more, are directly addressed by people at grassroots level, outside the mainstream. Solutions include, for instance, squatting and low impact living spaces, camps and campaigns throwing up fresh ideas and energy on eco-issues, an emphasis on self-empowerment through social acts like protest, free parties and newspapers, new music experiences and independent alternative media. (McKay, 1998: 53)

Both Studio één and MTK fit well within this framework. The activities of both labs were not isolated but tailored to fit within a larger framework of practical alternatives to institutional and/or corporate solutions. A 'temporary autonomous zone' (Bey, 1985: 1) was established in order to make an alternative way of living and working possible. Knowledge was freely exchanged between partner organisations, and newcomers were actively supported in creating their own spaces and workshops. Instead of standalone workplaces, the labs were part of a broader alternative infrastructure. An example is the masonry oven at le 102, built by the occupants in the event space. The oven provided warmth and food for the artists and visitors, creating a nurturing and welcoming environment for all. Similarly, the printing and editing facilities of Studio één were located in a miniature house in the back of a grand garden surrounding the main squat. Visiting artists would enter the grounds, walk down a path lined with trees, and find themselves in a colourful space that functioned both as kitchen and office. The activities of the lab were advertised with a flyer that was printed at KNUST press, an affiliated risograph collective also functioning on a not-for-profit basis (Extrapool, n.d.).

This form of community-focused enterprise provided a nurturing environment for the production of experimental film work that was made with the equipment the labs acquired – equipment that could be operated by the artists themselves. The importance of this approach is that the technical elements of film production were integrated within the creative process. In commercial film production, technical elements such as developing and printing are supposed to be invisible in order to achieve what is considered 'realism'. Perfection of the technical process is key in order to eliminate visible traces of the material and editing process. This technical protocol makes it possible to control colour, density, and exposure with utmost precision. In experimental film, these elements are often foregrounded. Therefore, it is a great advantage for the filmmakers to be in charge of this process themselves. The work of Cellule d'Intervention Metamkine is exemplary. Beyond their creative use of chemical manipulation and optical printing, the group also manipulates the film during projection, both revealing and mystifying their process under the gaze of the audience. On their website, the following statement can be found: 'The work is not theoretical. It's completely empirical. One of us offers the sound, the others the images. The important moment is the confrontation on stage' (Metamkine, n.d.) The confrontation that is mentioned here is both between the sound and the image and between the performers and the audience. Sound and image follow their own logic, interweaving and colliding with each other in a constant play of attraction and opposition. The sonic and the visual interchange, the result being a soundscape that can be 'seen' and visual music that can be 'listened to'. The audience is plunged into darkness, blinded by sudden bursts of light, teased by almost inaudible sounds, and deafened by raw Musique Concrète. Attending a Metamkine performance is first and foremost a physical experience: energetic and astonishing, ultimately bringing the spectators in a state of heightened physicality so they become aware of their own heartbeats, bloodstreams, and visual and auditory systems. The group's influences can be traced back to the work of earlier experimental filmmakers such as José Antonio Sistiaga and Patrick Bokanowski. The Spanish/Basque painter Sistiaga is known for his hand-painted films and in particular for the feature length 35mm film … *ere erera baleibu izik subua aruaren* … (1970). The film is made entirely without a camera by painting directly on the surface of the film, and it counteracts the idea that objective experience is a defining aspect of cinema. Sistiaga's film offers a subjective and handmade reality instead:

Sistiaga's welter of shifting, pulsating colours commingles representations of interiority and exteriority, and is at once a depiction of a cosmic circulatory system as well as the ring synapses of a galactic mind. The film is also rife with metaphoric tendencies, as hints of landscape and natural phenomena (the flow of electrons, snowstorms) enter and leave the frame. (Zinman, 2014: 171)

This quote also sheds light on the relationship between Sistiaga's work and Metamkine's performances with its mention of ringing synapses and natural phenomena. Without much imagery of landscape or nature, Metamkine succeeds in evoking a sense of the phenomenal quality offered by a profound experience such as waking up during a thunderstorm at night or descending from a mountain in a snowstorm. By exposing the audience alternating sudden bursts of light and sound and hypnotic sequences of whirling colours and buzzing drones, a state of disorientation is achieved. In this state, the spectator loses their sense of scale and time, which results in a mingling of interiority and exteriority. A second important influence can be found within the work of the French experimental filmmaker Patrick Bokanowski. In Bokanowski's short films and in his feature film *L'Ange* (1982), the optical and mechanical foundations of the motion picture camera are disrupted through the use of distorting lenses and mirrors and the manipulation of time. Refraction and reflection are used in order to look anew at quotidian scenes like bathers on the seaside, a woman preparing a meal in a kitchen, and librarians at work (see figure 2.2). The strangeness of the distorted images recasts these otherwise unremarkable scenes in a fascinating otherworldly way, arousing a parallel absurd or magical reality. In *L'Ange*, the characters and sets draw inspiration from astrology. The grotesque figures appear like automata trapped in repetitive actions. Time does not flow in a single direction but is interrupted, reversed, and suddenly lurches forward again. While Bokanowski achieves this surreal experience of time through ingenious postproduction, Metamkine introduces a live element to achieve something similar.

Not only do Auger and Quérel rework their sequences on a JK optical printer, but during projection the flow of images is decelerated, accelerated, and intermitted. In an early edition of their projection performance, a recurring image appears of a man sitting in an enclosed courtyard surrounded by tables and other pieces of furniture on which stacks of paper rest. The man takes a stack and throws it up in the air, filling the space with dozens of sheets flying around in all directions. In the background, windows and doorways are suddenly lit by bright light without any clear purpose or pattern. These images are manipulated by means of

Figure 2.2 *L'Ange* – Patrick Bokanowski (FR 1982, 35mm film, colour, 70min); courtesy of the artist.

optical printing: the man stands up time and time again, the paper flies in chaos; this is slowed down, reversed, and the paper returns in neat stacks. Explosive moments are alternated with serene slow motion, and through repetition of the action, a hypnotic effect is achieved. In projection, this sequence is again manipulated, duplicated, and warped. Thus, in Metamkine's live performances, projection is not used as a way to reproduce the filmed scenes in an automated way, but the role of the projection device is on par with the one usually reserved for musical instruments:

The projector is normally viewed as a practical necessity rather than a creative tool, less variable than the camera, lens, filmstrip, or optical printer. But the discourses of filmmakers who engage in projection performance are replete with references to the liberation of the projector from its role as automatic reproduction machine and projectionists as merely passive operator or overseer. (Walley, 2020: 205)

From these observations, a coherent view of Metamkine's methodology emerges: from beginning to end, their work is based on empirical forms of practice. Images are gathered rather than pre-planned in sequence, risks are taken with the chemical manipulations of footage, optical printing is used to make a number of variations of the same sequence, and finally, projection is the ultimate creative moment where sound and image come together. In Metamkine's projection performances, the projectors are positioned on stage, in full sight of the audience, throwing images on the screen via angled mirrors. Film reels, loops, hole punches, filters, torches, and other tools are scattered around the projectors within grasp of the performers (see figure 2.3). This is the realm of improvisation, extended to cinema. This certainly does not mean that there is no clear concept or idea. Bruce Bailey comments on the pejorative use of the word 'improvised' in a relevant way:

There is noticeable reluctance to use the word and some improvisors express a positive dislike for it. I think this is due to its widely accepted connotations which imply that improvisation is something without preparation and without considerations, a completely ad hoc activity, frivolous and inconsequential, lacking in design and method. (Bailey, 1980: xii)

Instead of lacking in design and method, a precise strategy pervades the whole production process: the building in which the artist's lab is based is renovated with recuperated materials, machines are second-hand and often repurposed for the artist's needs, and chemistry is used to create

Figure 2.3 *Cellule d'Intervention Metamkine* (FR 2018, expanded cinema performance); courtesy of www.ursss.com.

unconventional colours and textures. Taken together, these strategies create a genuinely independent space, not reliant on institutions, funding bodies, or protocols. What is at stake here is a free, autonomous form of cinema. To go back to Sistiaga, when ... *ere erera baleibu izik subua aruaren* ... was made, Spain was under Francoist dictatorship and it was forbidden to use the Basque language in public. Sistiaga's solution was to give the film a title that has no established meaning in any language. Giving too much weight to this nonsensical title would have led to an embarrassing situation for the authorities, and therefore no action was taken. For the public, however, it was perfectly clear that the title did express a Basque sensibility. This simple gesture shows how certain artistic choices can express autonomy without making manifest political statements. This rebellious yet 'nonaligned' attitude is also present in the production methods and live performances of Metamkine.

In this line of practice, the laboratory, with its developing, printing, and editing facilities, was and is a creative space for me. In my film *Meni* (1992), editing and printing are formative techniques central to the work. The film started with an improvised and completely self-directed dance sequence performed by Channa Wijmans. Her improvisation was inspired by the African dance classes she had been following. She handed me a cassette tape with music that would guide her movements, identifying the basic rhythm as 'Meni', hence the title of the film. I had cleared the floor in my living space and set up basic lighting, placing the two floods I had on both sides of the room. I shot a single roll of Super 8 film and, after processing, selected a twenty-five-second sequence (see figure 2.4). After studying the filmstrip frame by frame, I divided this sequence into short sections, each comprising a particular movement of the dancer's arms. I measured the sections and inserted black leader in order to make all of these equal in length. This short reel was copied seven times on Studio één's Super 8 contact printer. Now the editing process started again. First I neatly rearranged the shots in their initial order, and subsequently I exchanged shots, disrupting the rigid repetition. The moment I was satisfied with the level of disruption, I copied the film again. During this final step, I double-exposed the film, starting the second run about a second later. This procedure was very much influenced by the technical options that were available to me and the desire to experiment with the possibilities at hand. The project

Figure 2.4 *Meni* – Karel Doing (NL 1992 Super 8 film, bw, 3min).

started without a preconceived plan and developed step by step, and each time I closely observed and analysed the results of the previous step before proceeding further. This methodology of spontaneous action followed by close observation, analysis, restructuring, and synthesis has been defining throughout much of my work.

Looking back at this film, it is important to reflect on my use of 'African' dance and music. As described, the initial dance sequence was spontaneously filmed based on enthusiasm rather than critical thinking. During the further editing and copying of the film, the relationship between image and sound was the focus of my practical investigation. I was exploring gesture, repetition, and polyrhythm and using the above-described process of copying, editing, and superimposing as creative tools to achieve a sense of connection between moving, making, seeing, and hearing. To my mind, I was paying tribute to a musical genre that I liked and respected. However, my knowledge of that same music was very limited, and I did use the blanket term 'African drum' to describe the soundtrack. Kofi Agawu provides a highly relevant critical reflection in his article 'The Invention of "African Rhythm".' Firstly he points out that 'a continent with a population of upward 400 million distributed into forty-two countries and speaking some thousand languages is virtually unrecognizable in the unanimist constructions that some researchers have used in depicting African music' (Agawu, 1995: 384).

Secondly, he focuses on West African language and music, and more specifically Ewe language and music. Strikingly, there is no word for rhythm in Ewe, Tiv, Vai, and Hausa (the last being the most widely spoken sub-Saharan African language). Agawu points out that 'instead related concepts of stress, duration and periodicity do in fact register in subtle ways in Ewe discourse.' Furthermore, Agawu proposes that 'Ewe conceptions of rhythm often imply a binding together of different dimensional processes, a joining rather than separating, an across-the-dimensions rather than a within-the-dimensions phenomenon' (ibid., 388). Such a conception 'across-the-dimensions' does apply to my film, and while I was naive in terms of critical thinking, the work is more thorough in terms of practical implementation.

This improvisational approach and experimentation with printing and editing was also the focus of my next project, the film *Lichtjaren* (1993). For this project, I worked on three layers that were superimposed, using both the Super 8 contact printer and the Super 8 to 16mm printer. The first layer was a short sequence I filmed at night, cycling through the city and pointing my camera at the artificial lights along my route. I printed this sequence repeatedly, producing a pattern of coloured dots and stripes moving across the screen. The second layer was made by painting with household bleach on black leader, resulting in white and blue streaks and bubbles. The third part was made by setting up a camera in my living space using the long-exposure setting. In front of the camera, I created improvised movements with torches, candles, light bulbs, a flood light, and a small television set. Before I made the final print, I edited the three layers carefully in such a way that the total effect would be a supplementation rather than a cancelling out (see figure 2.5). While I was working on this project, one of the visiting artists was Joost Rekveld, who was studying sonology at the Royal Conservatory in The Hague. He was working on his film *#2*, described on his website as 'an early attempt to develop a form of

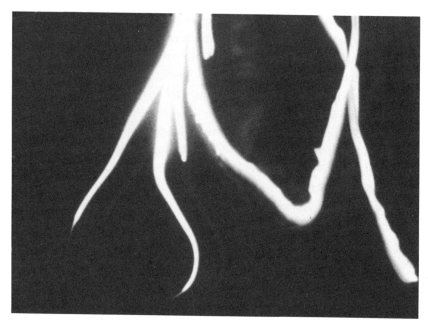

Figure 2.5 *Lichtjaren* – Karel Doing (NL 1993, Super 8 film, colour, 7min).

composition of light in time, comparable to the way sound is structured in a musical piece' (Rekveld, 2006). While he was working at Studio één, we had lively conversations about experimental film, music, and performance. I asked him to compose a soundtrack for my new film, given the fact that we were both interested in the interaction between image and sound. The resulting soundtrack is based on radio signals that were processed and arranged at the Institute of Sonology's electronic music studio.

Although the two forms of music used in *Meni* and *Lichtjaren* are hard to compare, both projects answer a similar line of inquiry. Instead of writing a script, meticulously planning shooting, focusing on continuity and narrative during the editing process, and using the lab as a purely technical resource, my approach to filmmaking diverted from the prevalent course of action from beginning to end. Shooting was spontaneous and in both cases focused on a physical performance. The representation of the body is not psychodramatic but rather investigates the body's relationship to space, time, light, and sound. Editing is subsequently used as a technique to analyse and restructure the results that were obtained. Finally, printing is used as a further creative element, reframing the image within a cinematic framework that answers to a distinct set of rules. This approach is also present in the work of Metamkine, with the addition of projection performance. The appearance of the body is not restricted to the filmstrip but is present in the form of haunting shadows cast on the screen by the filmmakers/performers. Shadows of hands and heads are either deliberately produced by flashes of torchlight or accidentally appear in the shifting beams of the projectors. Even the shadow of the audience is frequently used as an image that merges with the other elements on the screen.

A similar set of foundational principles is reflected within the broader artist-run film lab network. Many filmmakers who are part of this community are focused on a purely practise-based form of filmmaking that is driven in part or in full by the creative opportunities that an independent laboratory practice offers. Happy accidents are embraced during a journey of discovery that aims to explore new, forgotten, and underused possibilities of the analog film medium. Instead of the targeted rebellious character of the work described in chapter 1, the focus is rather on an autonomous and free form of filmmaking that refuses to define itself as oppositional against a mainstream. Instead, mainstream cinema is simply seen as irrelevant. The pointedness of this approach is finely worded by the anarchist author and poet Peter Lamborn Wilson (under his pen name Hakim Bey): 'Only the autonomous can *plan* autonomy, organize for it, create it. It's a bootstrap operation' (Bey, 1985: 96).

3

A New Form of Beauty

In 1993, my film *Meni* was selected for the European Media Art Festival (EMAF) in Osnabrück, Germany. This festival grew out of a platform for experimental film, organised by the University of Osnabrück, and provided a lively and supportive environment for the media arts (EMAF, 2021). Besides the main film and video program, the festival also offered installations and multimedia performances. Without knowing what to expect, I decided to attend *Circus of the Senses* (1993), an expanded cinema performance by the British collective Loophole Cinema. A crowd gathered in front of a defunct steel factory and was led into an empty hall. The steel doors were shut from the outside, leaving the audience in almost-complete darkness, long enough for them to get used to the low light conditions and also long enough to for them to get impatient for the show to start. Eventually, a smaller door opened to the next space, disclosing a factory hall divided in half by a large projection screen. Low melodious sounds were interspersed with clanging metal. Flashes of light started to appear on the screen, revealing geometric shapes, warped forms, and shadows cast by hands. The light show grew in intensity, revealing glimpses of the silhouettes of the performers and adding high-contrast black-and-white film projections into the mix. Slowly the overhead crane started moving, transporting the screen first toward and subsequently over the heads of the assembled crowd. While the screen was moving, the images projected from the far side of the space grew, and the images projected over the backs of the audience shrank. As a result of this intervention, the entire spatial ratio of the machine hall seemed to change. Performers dressed in boiler suits walked around the room, starting up additional machinery. Two powerful industrial ventilators were lit by stroboscopes, rendering the rotators stationary in the perception of the public while the whirring of the motors and the streams of air could be heard and felt. After the screen had moved back and forth, the audience was invited to enter another hall, featuring an installation with elongated projections on screens that were installed in the shape of a funnel, temporarily trapping the audience before they could make their way toward the exit. Finally, the spectators found themselves outside again, surrounded by industrial wasteland. The performers guarded bright fires in empty oil drums while melancholic music could still be heard coming from the abandoned factory.

The core members of the group were performer and filmmaker Greg Pope, technologist Ivan Pope, installation artist and filmmaker Bea Haut, multimedia artist and musician Paul Rodgers, and electronic musician Ben Hayman. The composition of the group differed for each performance and included a number of guest artists, musicians, and performers of various breeds. Prior to this large-scale event, the group had realised a number of site-specific performances and installations. One of the first Loophole Cinema events was called *Effects of Darkened Rooms* (1990), a performance in an industrial basement located in Glasgow on Renfrew Street next to the Centre for Contemporary Arts (now Glasgow Film Theatre). The performance space was close to the main exhibition venue, but at the same time separated from it, which later turned out to be a perfect arrangement for the group's performances. A 'shadow maze' was set up in the basement, creating a performative installation with multiple screens and a dozen Super 8 projectors. The festival program included this quote from Greg Pope: 'people wandering around being bombarded with images, they kind of edit their own film' (Hunter, 1990). A different approach was adopted during the performance *Vacant Procession* (1993) that took place in a twenty-storey tower block in Birmingham that was scheduled for demolition. The audience was led to a central chamber of an empty flat, while members of the group started with a controlled demolition of the walls of the adjacent rooms. Flood lights were positioned behind the performers, and when a hole appeared in the wall, the light would hit the jumble of dust particles that was now flying around. When the hole grew larger, the silhouettes of the demolition crew became visible amid the dust. In the group's subsequent performances in abandoned factories, pools, theatres, and outdoor spaces, the concept of the 'shadow engineer' would remain a continuous element (see figure 3.1). In an interview conducted by me, Greg Pope states:

We had this phrase: shadow engineers and shadow engine. In the end we invented our little theory that a show would be like as if the audience could be shrunk and walked around inside a 16mm projector with all the cogs and shadows and lights cast. Being inside rather than outside. We were the little engineers scurrying around, keeping the cogs turning. (Doing, 2017: 174)

Besides their performances, the group also produced several installations such as *Propaganda Beacons* (1991), an installation that was built and exhibited downstairs in the London Filmmakers' Co-op, a former laundry, during the London Film Festival that year. This installation consisted of a number of portable turntables fitted with revolving, perforated cylinders through which light was transmitted back into the space. The turntables were concurrently playing second-hand records randomly chosen from a junk shop. As the needle approached the cylinder, it would get stuck and play the same groove over and over. The basic idea for the installation was to construct 'something that projects light and sound in synchronisation but is not film' (ibid., 160).

In contrast to the squatting movement's more permanent appropriation and reuse of abandoned industrial sites, Loophole Cinema's interventions were short-lived. But during these brief encounters, these uncared-for spaces were brought back to life in a unique way. The early Loophole Cinema performances coincided with the emergence of rave culture in the UK. Thatcher's radical right-wing politics had resulted in a sharp decline of industrial activities and the abandonment of many warehouses and factories. Early rave culture jumped into the gaping hole that was left in the urban fabric: 'As the subculture grew in popularity, it escaped the confines of the club circuit, occupying derelict warehouses, aircraft hangars and fields with innumerable parties every weekend' (John, 2015: 162). This occupation was only temporary and born out of aspirations different to the squatting movement. While the free party movement had an ideological grounding in collectivism and anti-consumerism, many party organisers had no altruistic motives and instead used the popularity of acid house music to earn large sums of money. Still, rave culture was seen as a threat to society: 'What made rave

Figure 3.1 *Shadow Engine* – Loophole Cinema (UK 1991, expanded cinema, 40min); photograph by Adam Pope.

culture before 1994 such a potent test of the Thatcherite political philosophy was its ability, in true heterotopic fashion, to simultaneously reflect and contest the ideologies of the dominant culture in a confusion of juxtaposing' (ibid.,180).

In London, the free party movement was connected to direct action manifestations such as the occupation of Claremont Road, the theatrical events organised by Reclaim the Streets, the punk performances of Mutoid Waste Company, and the open screenings organised by Exploding Cinema. These events brought together activists, artists and partygoers, amalgamating the political and the artistic with pure pleasure. Moreover, rave is often described as having a religious connection: 'embracing pre- or post-Christian communions, post-rave pundits champion the "shamanic" states of consciousness engendered or "trance" states triggered by the new ritual' (St John, 2014: 4). Analogous to this proposition, Loophole Cinema's performances resembled pagan processions, not only leading the audience through a set of spatial encounters but also inscribing meaning during the process, celebrating the cultural significance and monumentality of the architectural sites. Loophole Cinema's performances did also incorporate trance, inducing stroboscopic lights and projections, and electronically stored samples that were looped and layered in order to produce hypnotic soundscapes.

Besides these coincidences of practical, spatial, and aesthetic elements that were also present in early Rave culture, Loophole Cinema's site-specific work tapped into a different side of the zeitgeist. The performances took place on sites such as a defunct steelworks, and a tower block that was due to be demolished. The performers, who were dressed in boiler suits, were described in terms of 'shadow engineering'. Therefore, it is apt to compare the performances of Loophole Cinema with Test Dept, a musical group that was active from 1981 to 1997 (coming back together in a new formation in 2016). In their early concerts, the group used repurposed industrial hammers and canisters as percussion instruments to create rousing rhythms. Black-and-white films were projected showing the band members as heroic 'shock workers' deliberately summoning up a Soviet-style 'cinema of attractions'. In their graphic design, the band used a style that was heavily influenced by the compositions of Alexander Rodchenko. The group expressed their solidarity with the miners' strike by organising benefit concerts and collaborating with colliery choirs and brass bands. Independent scholar Tim Forster proposes that 'this use of Constructivist aesthetics explicitly identified the collaboration of Test Dept and the miners with the historic experience of class struggle' (Forster, 2022: 238). In contrast, Loophole Cinema's performances did not express clear political viewpoints. The group did use Soviet-inspired graphic design, most notably on the flyers that were created for the installation *Propaganda Beacons* (see figure 3.2). The name for the installation was inspired by the idea that early Soviet cinema functioned as a propaganda machine for the communist revolution. But the resulting installation was rather Dadaist, offering a disorienting experience in sound and image that literally made the heads of the audience spin. The appearance of engineers in boiler suits in Loophole Cinema's performances did not convey such a clear-cut message as the communist shock worker revived by the Test Dept performers. In Loophole Cinema's performances the workers did not appear as heroic individuals but rather as benevolent participants who were keeping the grand architectural and cinematic spectacle working, having only partial control over the machinery. While Test Dept's activities are clearly aimed at 'the historic experience of class struggle', Loophole Cinema's performances are rather reflective of the contested transformation of the working class as a unifying identity:

By the early 1980s, the class-centered politics of the socialist tradition was in crisis. In this situation, leading commentators took on apocalyptic tones. By the end of the 1980s, the Left remained deeply divided between the advocates of change ('New Times' required new politics) and the defenders of the faith (class politics could be practiced, mutatis mutandis, much as before). (Eley & Nield, 2000: 1)

Loophole Cinema's shadow engineers offered neither a revival of the traditional working-class hero nor a figure that was in any way inspired by Tony Blair's 'third way' politics that started to take shape when he was elected as leader of the Labour party in 1994. Instead, the shadow engineers operated in a loophole, in a spatial and perceptual ambiguity that became visible through the group's cinematographic interventions in the derelict buildings. Therefore, their performances might be better understood as a

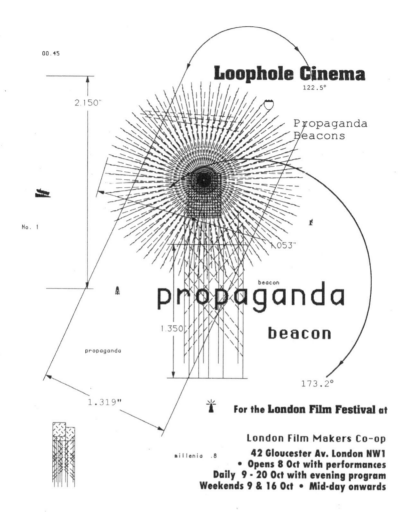

Figure 3.2 *Propaganda Beacons* – Loophole Cinema (UK 1991, flyer); courtesy of Ivan Pope.

broader comment on architecture and the urban experience rather than as a comment on British society.

From a modernist, objective, and rational point of view, the moment that a building ceases to have a function, its value disappears. However, a new function can manifest in a number of different ways, for example, through the transformation of a former industrial site into living quarters, a museum or an entertainment hub. In the period in between these stages, the building is merely seen as an object without purpose, most emphatically as a symbol for a past era that can be transformed into a monument. But seen through the eyes of the creative practitioner, such a building can reveal unseen possibilities. In his article about industrial architecture and negativity, writer and urbanist Maroš Krivý discusses three case studies: the photographs of Bernd and Hilla Becher, the sculptural interventions of Gordon Matta-Clark, and the landscape photography of Robert Smithson. Bernd and Hilla Becher are known for their photographs of cooling towers, blast furnaces, and other industrial objects, which document these anonymous constructions shortly before they become defunct. In the writer's discussion of these photographs, the idea of negativity in architecture is defined:

When precisely edited and rigorously arranged into grids, we see in these industrial objects some formal and material 'surplus' that cannot be explained simply by reference to their function. This is the negativity of industrial architecture, the non-functional 'excess' beyond its functionality. No two industrial objects are actually the same, in spite of being engineering works of pure functionality. (Krivý, 2010: 845)

Bernd and Hilla Becher's approach is minimalist and non-interventional, but their work does demonstrate that these structures can call forth a form of poetry when seen through the right lens. In a similar fashion, the 'anarchitect' Gordon Matta-Clark transformed an ordinary Parisian apartment into a dazzling sculpture. In his work *Conical Intersect* (1975), he reveals a negative space by cutting away sections of walls, ceilings, and floors in order to create an imaginary conical form inside the apartment. *Conical Intersect* referred to the expanded cinema work *Line Describing a Cone* (1973) by Anthony McCall. 'In both McCall's film and Matta-Clark's building, a reference to optics – a cone of vision – is shaped by a literalized absence' (Lee, 2000: 176). Matta-Clark's work provoked strong emotions by upturning the deeply rooted architectural tenets of the spectators: 'The normal coordinates of architectural orientation were interrupted to such a degree that a sense of vertigo was produced for the observer inside the building' (ibid., 171). Krivý's third case study focuses on land artist Robert Smithson, who reveals a monumentality that is hidden in plain sight in his series of six photographs titled *The Monuments of Passaic* (1967). The pictures show seemingly random architectural objects that would normally not be seen as having any significance. By framing and presenting these objects as monuments, the artist draws attention to the fact that 'a monument is not only a statue in the middle of a square, but also a quarry which provides the necessary material for its construction' (Krivý, 2010: 840). All three case studies question the modernist utilitarian conception by questioning the axioms of architecture. Suddenly a blast furnace, a partially demolished apartment, and a building pit reveal undisclosed formal and ontological aspects of architectural design and space.

During the preparation of their performances, Loophole Cinema surveyed each site in order to reconfigure the spatial and temporal experiences that the spectator would encounter. By either obstructing the view of an open space or by revealing a new view of an enclosed space, Loophole Cinema throw the expectations of the audience into confusion. Simultaneously, shadow projections would complicate the matter, interfering with the ordinary perceptions of size. A hand appears as an enormous object, superimposed with the silhouette of a person. Small objects fill the entire screen, and a moment later reappear much smaller, distorted by optics. The layering of film projection, shadow projection, and in some cases live-video feeds complicate an immediate understanding of the separate components of the moving image. Through the use of samples of prerecorded sounds alongside sonic interventions, a similar aural experience was created. Moving a screen, cutting through a wall, or opening a hidden door could change spatial perception once more. Repetitive sounds and images, stroboscopic lights, and humming and rumbling machinery all contributed to a sense of perceptual disorientation. Performative, cinematic, and architectural elements fused into an overall experience, destabilising the spectator's conception of spatial and temporal relations. Greg Pope confirmed the connection with the work of Gordon Matta-Clark and Anthony McCall in the above-mentioned interview. Talking about the performance *Vacant Procession*, he said: 'We are in the very outside two chambers drilling through with very strong lights behind us, and that creates an image, the dust, it is a bit like *Line*

Describing a Cone pure punky' (Doing, 2017: 181). The raw material taken up by Loophole Cinema – a former steelworks, an unloved apartment in a tower block, or a grubby basement – transmogrified into a playground for the senses, challenged the spectator's notion of architectural redundancy. Instead of the modernist notion of purpose, hypercharged by Thatcher's neoliberalism, these architectural spaces became playgrounds of resistance. This approach brings to mind the writing of cultural theorist Johan Huizinga:

Play can be deferred or suspended at any time. It is never imposed by physical necessity or moral duty. It is never a task. It is done at leisure, during 'free time'. Only when play is a recognized cultural function – a rite, a ceremony – is it bound up with notions of obligation and duty. Here then, we have the first main characteristic of play: that it is free, is in fact freedom. A second characteristic is closely connected with this, namely, that play is not 'ordinary' or 'real' life. It is rather a stepping out of 'real' life into a temporary sphere of activity with a disposition all of its own. (Huizinga, 2016: 8)

The notion of 'stepping out of real life' captures Loophole Cinema's performances well. Not only were the projections and sounds imaginative but the reconfiguration of the architectural space itself resulted in the creation of a speculative arena where day-to-day rules were suspended. This conjunction of architecture and play brings to mind the unitary urbanism program of the Situationist International, an international group of radical thinkers and practitioners that was formed in 1957: 'Unitary urbanism rejected the utilitarian logic of the consumer society, aiming instead for the realisation of a dynamic city, a city in which freedom and play would have a central role' (Heynen, 1996: 25). One of the members of the Situationist International, the Dutch artist Constant Nieuwenhuis, dedicated all his energy to a new project that he named *New Babylon* (1956–1974), a series of models, maps, and paintings that prefigure the realisation of unitary urbanism. In this body of work, Constant envisioned an elevated city covering the globe, an interlinked network of endless corridors, bridges, ladders, and so-called spatiovores: 'Resembling space stations accidentally landed on earth, transparent shell-shaped structures rise high above the ground' (ibid., 29). *New Babylon*'s citizens would be able to focus entirely on creativity, love, and play, while all necessary labour would be taken over by machines. People would have no fixed address and live like nomads, travelling through the network, indefinitely reconfiguring spaces and social relationships in the process. Notwithstanding the clear utopian nature of his vision, a tension between light and dark is continuously present in Constant's work: 'The drawings and paintings show a condition in which wanderlust and freedom from permanent ties are untrammelled, but they also make evident that this condition is inseparably bound up with the death drive, with groundlessness and indeterminacy' (ibid., 38).

Loophole Cinema's shadow engineers suggest a similar contradiction, first by appearing only as shadows, superimposed with each other, appearing and disappearing in the blink of an eye. But also, when the screen is drawn and the shadow engineers reveal themselves, their boiler suits provide a de-personified, uniform impression. Furthermore, hands, silhouettes, and objects are projected in a great variety of sizes, taking advantage of the spacious performance area behind the screen. A single hand can dominate almost the entire screen, appearing as a manifestation of more-than-human power. Their playful and in some cases humorous performances produced a darker, eerie, and grotesque experience as well. By combining these contradictory elements, Loophole Cinema's performances impart not only a sense of thrill, disorientation, and surprise, but also melancholy and humour. Such a combination of horror, play, and melancholy can also be found in the installation *Théâtre d'ombres* (1985–1990) by Christian Boltanski, named by Loophole Cinema's Greg Pope as one of their important influences. In his installations, Boltanski uses small cut-out metal figures of skeletons, skulls, and fallen angels suspended in a wireframe. A ventilator ensures gentle movement, and projectors illuminate the figures casting enormous dancing shadows on the walls of the exhibition space.

There is a tender humor in the images. The shadows frighten, but they are, at the same time, sweet, they are toy artifacts, they exhibit the malleability of the game, they appear and disappear with fear, they come and go with it, routinely, because they are the offspring of oblivion. (Kohl Bines, 2015: 137)

Boltanski refers to both the theatricality and the fragility of the shadow. The shadow is a trick that can be used to impress the spectator. Simultaneously, shadows are ephemeral, appearing and disappearing in an instance. In Loophole Cinema's performances, shadows are produced, creating a giant machine in which both the engineers/performers and the spectators wander. Ultimately, it is not this speculative situation that is frightening but rather the reality of modernist utilitarianism that renders buildings, jobs, and people obsolete in the name of progress. The performance *Vacant Procession* can again serve as an example, demonstrating how the imaginative use of an unloved apartment in a tower block can become an uplifting antidote against sorrowful social deprivation. Instead of cultural activism, Loophole Cinema was more of a 'hearts and minds' operation, providing an enchanting remedy against cold and calculating neoliberal thinking. The group briefly resisted the steamrolling engine of a ferocious urban renewal project in disregard of people and planet. Their site-specific performances brought cinema, music, performance and architecture together, creating something new from the scrapheap.

The theme of ferocious urban renewal without any regard for people and planet also appears in the work of San Francisco–based filmmaker Dominic Angerame. In 1984, Angerame started working on a series of films under the umbrella title *City Symphony*, a well-known trope that is mainly associated with major modernist films such as *Berlin, Symphonie einer Großstad* by Walter Ruttmann (1927), and *Man with a Movie Camera / Человек с Киноаппаратом* by Dziga Vertov (1929). But Angerame's films are notably different in that their focus is on urban transience. An analysis in the long-running *Millennium Film Journal* connects Angerame's films with the mindset of Austrian political economist Joseph Schumpeter:

Angerame's version of the city symphony is peculiarly interesting in that he so perfectly illustrates the ideas of one of Ruttmann's more prescient contemporaries, Joseph Schumpeter. Lately in vogue after long obscurity, Schumpeter called capitalism a form of 'creative destruction', in which innovation overwhelms and erases that which preceded it. (Frye, 2003: 105–106)

This approach is clearly articulated in two films that were made during the first half of the 1990s; *Deconstruction Site* (1990) and *Premonition* (1995). Angerame uses bright overexposed whites and deep saturated blacks to show an ever-changing cityscape. On both sides of this tonal range, his bold use of high-contrast black-and-white film complicates a straightforward reading of the photographic image. Sunny spots and reflections are 'burned out', while deep shadows create mysterious voids. Additionally, Angerame recurrently uses the variable shutter of his Bolex camera to reveal and obscure the image, starting from a bright, overexposed scene and closing the shutter until the image is completely black. Furthermore, images are superimposed, creating an intricate meshwork of entangled lines, textures, and volumes. His framing is deliberately fragmented, depicting slivers and shards of objects, buildings, vehicles. The bodies of workers and pedestrians are often shown only partially: a pair of legs crossing the street, the body of a worker on the edge of the frame, a silhouette blending into the shadow of a large construction. *Deconstruction Site* starts with a quote from the influential artist and photographer László Moholy-Nagy: 'Since the industrial revolution our civilization has suffered from a growing discrepancy between ideological potentiality and actual realization' (Moholy-Nagy, 1947: 13). The film starts with images of workers, cranes, crumbling brick walls, the tracks of a tramway, and pedestrians hurrying across the street, before proceeding to a sequence focused on a construction site, which is filmed with a long lens. Construction workers can be seen wandering through cage-like metal frames, while helmeted welders appear like aliens lit up by peculiar bright sparks (see figure 3.3). Images of a crew of firemen extinguishing a smouldering fire on a rooftop are superimposed

Figure 3.3 *Deconstruction Site* – Dominic Angerame (US 1990, 16mm film, bw, 12min); courtesy of the artist.

with otherworldly images of a waterfall. This water sequence is contin- ued with shots of water flowing under the famous Golden Gate Bridge. Here, the film segues into a longer sequence depicting a demolition site. The half-demolished building appears like a weeping willow, its innards sadly hanging downward while cranes chomp relentlessly. This sequence is punctuated by sped-up images of office towers at night, with clouds, unnaturally lit by city light, rushing by in the background. Finally, the images of the demolition are also sped up, giving an impression of inevi- table decline. This haunted cityscape reappears in *Premonition*. This time Angerame's camera focuses on the deserted Embarcadero Freeway, a monumental elevated road between the Bay Bridge and the Golden Gate Bridge. This freeway suffered major damage as a result of the 1989 earth- quake, and after many heated political debates, the enormous construc- tion was taken down. *Premonition* starts with shots of the giant concrete pillars with cars driving underneath. Slowly, the camera moves further up, showing the empty elevated road. The camera explores the surround- ing cityscape, alternating between close-ups and wide shots, occasionally showing human activity. Upon the camera's return to the empty freeway, an eerie feeling starts to sink in, brought forth by the absence of traffic. For a further understanding of such an 'eerie' experience connected to an oth- erwise ordinary urban space, Mark Fisher's precise analysis of the word is relevant: 'The eerie, by contrast, is constituted by a *failure of absence* or by a *failure of presence*. The sensation of the eerie occurs either when there is something present where there should be nothing, or if there is noth- ing present when there should be something' (Fisher, 2016: 61). Following this line of thought, a 'failure of presence' in *Premonition* is mirrored by a 'failure of absence' in Gordon Matta-Clark's *Conical Intersect*. Analogous to the missing traffic, the cone-shaped hole in the vacant Parisian apartment brings up questions about agency. If the road feels strange without cars and the apartment is even weirder as a result of the sculptural interven- tion, what or who exactly is the driving force of normality? We are so used to perceiving our built environment through the lens of a utilitarian point of view that the moment this is distorted, a feeling of confusion, anxiety or (on the positive side) wonder is triggered.

In conclusion, it is clear that the work of Loophole Cinema and Dominic Angerame, as well as the previously described canonical artworks, are concerned with the perception of architectural objects and interior space, while simultaneously digging deeper into questions about value, loss, identity, and memory. The performances of Loophole Cinema provide for the pure enjoyment of otherwise unloved spaces like the defunct steelworks in Osnabrück or the apartment in Birmingham due to be demolished. The performances are realised with a mixed set of tools, respectively related to engineering and cinema. On the engineering side, their tools include an overhead crane, industrial ventilators, drills, sledgehammers, and utility flashlights. On the cinema side, we find 16mm film projectors, lenses, screens, apertures, and stroboscopic effects. By concatenating these two domains, a new conception of architectural space becomes possible. Utility and imagination are combined in playful performances that can be freely explored by the spectators. The deteriorated, abandoned, and defunct spaces are revived temporarily, in a spectacle that relates not only to the original use of the premises but also to their cultural significance. These buildings will be lost, and with their deconstruction, a way of living also ceases to exist. But rather than mourning this loss, the performances create valuable memories in the minds of the spectators. Instead of the grinding machine of 'creative destruction' that has no regard for human values, the spectator participates in a final 'creative appropriation' of the architectural object. A similar mechanism is at work in Angerame's films. Construction and deconstruction are situated side by side, shiny surfaces are treated in the same way as crumbling textures, the freeway is simultaneously a monument and an object that is simply discarded. His films thus forge connections rather than separations. Here, the 'urban fabric' is not just another fancy term that describes the constantly changing environment of modern culture. Pure sensory and spatial awareness, cultural signification, and a deeper realisation of the cyclic nature of all things are woven together in a poetic, humane, but also unsettling portrait of the city. The 'discrepancy between ideological potentiality and actual realization' is what should bother us. Instead of being 'anti-progress' or nostalgic, both Loophole Cinema's performances and Dominic Angerame's work demonstrate how progress could be made in a unifying way, valuing the connections between architecture, cinema, identity, spirituality, memory, loss, and imagination.

4

Alchemy

In 1994, I was invited to screen my work at the London Filmmakers'
Co-op. At the time, the projectionist at this legendary organisation was Greg
Pope, one of the key members of Loophole Cinema. We became friends
and started to collaborate in a number of different ways. In the winter of
1995, Pope was invited as an artist in residence at the artist studio complex Duende in Rotterdam, where my lab was based as well. Studio één had
moved from Arnhem to Rotterdam earlier that year, attracted by the large
studio, the low rent, and the lively cultural climate. The city actively pro-
moted itself as a hub for artists and filmmakers. Duende provided a roof
for more than forty artist studios, plus two guest studios that were housed
in several interconnected former school buildings. Pope's residency took
place during the winter months, which turned out to be much colder than
usual, and even the broad river Maas partially froze. Pope had brought some
rolls of high-contrast 16mm film and undertook regular trips to the harbour
in his blue Mini Cooper, taking advantage of the bright and low winter sun.
We developed the film by hand, which made it possible to see the results
shortly after shooting. We printed the camera negative – using Studio één's
printer – for a performance that was due to take place at the end of his residency. We projected multiple images of wind turbines, cranes, refineries,
buoys, and ships on a large screen in an empty studio, accompanied by a
soundtrack that we had recorded earlier in the hallway, rolling empty film
cans and other objects back and forth through the echoing space. Pope's
images were compelling, and we decided to work on a single-screen version, using the footage to compile a short film that could be distributed further. The resulting film, *Maas Observation* (1997), starts with a rhythmical
sequence focused on a row of wind turbines located on the 'Maasvlakte',

a stretch of industrial land reclaimed from the North Sea. The turbines act as the shutter blades of a film projector, associating the two machines with each other. The turbines' rotating blades cast their long shadows on an eerily empty field. After this sequence, Pope's camera travels through the vast expanse of container terminals and refineries, playfully interacting with the surreal man-made landscape by hitchhiking on a crane, reversing the smoke that is perpetually coming out of a chimney, and photographing the slowly moving ships against the reflection of the sun on the water.

Not long after this collaboration, Loophole Cinema organised a large-scale event in London, the *International Symposium of Shadows* (1996). The group had gained access to the West India Quay Warehouses, a half-mile-long row of warehouses built at the beginning of the eighteenth century to store sugar, coffee, and rum produced by slave labour in the Caribbean colonies. Heavy wooden floors were interspersed with cast-iron studs, which gave the interior a distinct character (see further Hobhouse, 1994). I had brought my Bolex camera and asked my fellow artists to perform small actions, and I used long exposure to capture these in the available low-light conditions. In 1997, we collaborated again for the performance *Light Struck* in a former cigar factory in Breda that had been turned into an art venue. During the buildup to this performance, I shot more footage on expired 16mm colour negative. As we brought together this footage, with shots from London and further Super 8 material that was made during Pope's residency in Rotterdam, another collaborative project materialised, resulting in the film *Whirlwind* (1998). While for *Maas Observation* the film processing and film printing facilities at Studio één were primarily used as a way to work in a quick, direct, and spontaneous way, in *Whirlwind* the creative possibilities of these normally 'invisible' technical manipulations were explored much further. Colour reversal Super 8 film was 'cross processed', rendering a brightly coloured negative via swapping the E6 reversal chemistry for C41. Black-and-white reversal Super 8 film was processed with a graphic film developer, which resulted in a negative image with enhanced grain. The expired colour negative had to be processed on a lower temperature with special chemistry, to prevent the brittle emulsion from falling off entirely. Subsequently, the footage was reworked on a JK optical printer, including the bi-packing, looping, superimposing, and slowing down of selected shots. The resulting film is more than documentation: instead of a simple recording of Loophole Cinema's performance, a new cinematic spatial and temporal subjectivity is created based on the actions, sites, inventions, and tools used by the group and the invited guest artists.

An important frontrunner who has specialised in the use of chemical manipulation as a creative tool is the German filmmaker Jürgen Reble. As mentioned in chapter 2, Reble's performance and workshop during the AVE festival in Arnhem were crucial for the maturation of my own filmmaking practice. Reble had formerly been part of the collective *Schmelzdahin*, a group formed in 1980 by Jochen Lempert, Jochen Müller, and Reble himself. The group started using Super 8 in a playful way, discovering the material qualities of film by scratching the emulsion. The films were projected in combination with theatrical and funny interventions by the artists, mostly in a domestic setting. In 1984, the group made *Stadt in Flammen,* a film made with footage taken from a Canadian B-movie about a small city in turmoil (see figure 4.1). The film was made by throwing the original Super 8 footage in the garden and covering it with compost. After

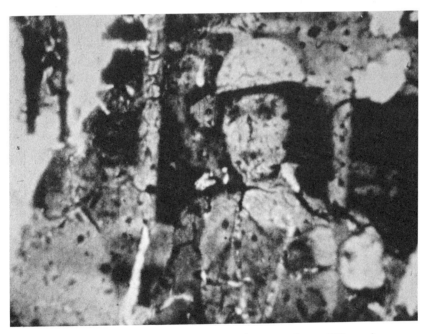

Figure 4.1 *Stadt in Flammen* – Schmelzdahin (DE 1984, Super 8 film, colour, 5min); courtesy of Jürgen Reble.

a period during which the film deteriorated, it was dug up and then treated with a sewing machine and a hole punch. After this treatment, an optical print of the film was made with a self-built optical printer. According to Reble, this procedure added another element to the film: 'You see images in a staccato, but the images are melting in a way, or melting together, by the heat of the lamp' (Doing, 2017: 109) A soundtrack was recorded on the magnetic stripe of the film during its first projection. The artists performed while watching the film: 'One of us was lying on the ground, looking at the image, and the other one was beating on the chest, in the same rhythm that the image was changing. It was a kind of comment on the film, as a kind of live act' (ibid.). Similar methods were used in *Aus den Algen* (1986), a film thrown into a fish pond where it was slowly covered with algae, and *Weltenempfanger* (1985), a film developed with rainwater and coffee waste. In 1989, Reble decided to go solo, driven by the desire to focus entirely on a more precise and controlled form of chemical manipulation. Together with sound artist and composer Thomas Köner, he toured with the performance *Alchemie* (1992). A 16mm film projector is loaded with a ten-metre-long film loop, previously developed and stop bathed. During the projection, the loop is led through a shallow bowl containing bleach or peroxide (see figure 4.2). The black parts of the image slowly disappear during the projection, leaving milky yellow parts. Subsequently, the remaining part of the image is developed, turning from milky yellow to black. The full-grown image is attacked with acid, which decays and eventually destroys the film. Köner amplified the sounds of the projector and the sizzling of the chemicals interacting with the film emulsion, placing the audience sonically *inside* the machine and the process, implicating them physically in the work. Reble describes the performance thusly: 'it is like giving birth, starting with an untouched image in the beginning and death in the end' (ibid., 116). The audience could experience a process that would normally take place in a darkroom. Not only is there a succession of frames producing an illusory movement on the screen, but there is also a real movement within the frame, produced by the enlarged chemical process that can be seen in action.

Reble mentions alchemy: 'The alchemistic idea is to change the structure of the molecules and the atoms, but not in a positivistic and natural science way, but by having a feeling or an intention that something is going

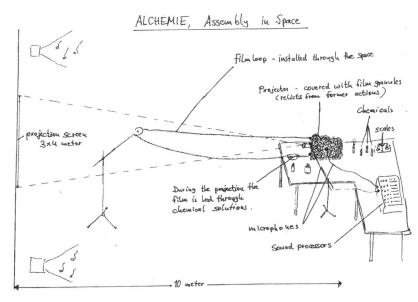

ALCHEMIE, Assembly in Space

Figure 4.2 *Alchemie* - Jürgen Reble & Thomas Köner (DE 1992, expanded cinema performance, 45min); courtesy of the artist.

on in the molecules' (ibid., 117). In the performance *Tabula Smaragdina* (1997), this theme is explored further. The title refers to a legendary tablet containing a text by the ancient Greek or Egyptian Hermes Trismegistus (of contested date, somewhere between 1800 BC and AD 800), who was highly regarded by the European alchemists, and the tablet is seen as the foundation of their art. In the performance, Reble uses three projectors, two 16mm and one 35mm, projecting overlapping images on the screen. The machines are not synchronised, and Reble manipulates the speed and the direction of each device. Thomas Köner wired the mechanisms with contact microphones and produced a soundtrack that is based on the interiority of the projectors. Reble's imagery is that of a pulsating sphere, changing from a seemingly liquid to a solid or gaseous form and back. Images of microscopic life forms, sea creatures, and grid-like structures emerge out of a seemingly chaotic mass of dots, flecks, and crystals (see figure 4.3). The images evoke both a microscopic and a macroscopic environment, leaving the viewers to choose their own path toward interpretation. The flickering,

Figure 4.3 *Tabula Smaragdina* – Jürgen Reble (DE 1997, expanded cinema performance, 45min); courtesy of the artist.

layering, slow changes and repetitive sounds induce a hypnotic effect, reminiscent of Ken Jacobs's *Nervous System* performances (1975–2000):

> The Nervous System plays on our nervous system. Jacobs not only operates his analytical projectors, he also hooks into our most primal processes of perception. Our basic ability to perceive figure and ground, movement out of stillness, to synthesize space and time are played with, as though we were hotwired to the screen. Space, motion, time, and imagery dance before us, eternally breaking apart and coming together. (Gunning, 2009)

In an interview conducted by Berkeley historian Harry Kreisler, Jacobs refers to cinema as a 'way of thinking, a way of conducting the mind, so it can be very dangerous' (Institute of International Studies at the University of California, Berkeley, 2008), suggesting that his explorations of the cinematic apparatus are primarily concerned with the critical dissection and reassembly of the medium. Both Reble and Jacobs are often described as 'magicians', which calls forth the popular interpretation of the figure of the alchemist. For a further analysis of Reble's work, it is therefore relevant to look closer at the history and principles of alchemy.

Michela Pereira, who has specialised in the subject, states that the aim of alchemy is 'to produce an agent of perfection which could transmute metals into gold and grant perfect health and even rejuvenation to human bodies' (Pereira, 2000a: 118) The alchemists believed in the unity of the divine, human, and natural world: 'It is this unity that makes human activity capable of penetrating the secret levels of all natural dynamics' (ibid., 119). This was achieved through 'a wisdom where theoretical knowledge is acquired and taught in close union with practice, indeed where knowledge is born from practice and not *vice versa*' (Pereira, 2000b: 132-133). It is not difficult to draw an analogy with experimental cinema in general and the work of Reble in particular. In motion picture film, silver is 'transmuted' by means of exposure and the subsequent chemical development of the latent image. The resulting images exhibit and preserve the motion and appearance of human activity to perfection. Notably, Reble's films and performances are focused on concrete natural phenomena. He frequently uses images of insects, birds, mammals, marine life, and microorganisms. These 'natural' scenes are intercut with quotidian scenes from his own surroundings, showing seemingly ordinary human activities. Human and animal appearances are complemented by shots that relate to either a scientific or spiritual realm, such as images from documentaries about space exploration, the birth of a child, the sun and the moon, or pulsating spheres. Taken together, these shots present to the spectator a holistic view of the universe in which nature and culture, technology and spirituality all exist coextensively. The chemical manipulation transforms the footage into moving emblems that merge in and out of abstraction. Recognisable images appear and disappear, coming out of a 'primal soup' and disintegrating into swarms of particles. Still, the chemical process itself is a concrete precipitation of a natural phenomenon. As we draw these parallels, it becomes evident that Reble's references to alchemy are far from gratuitous. His extensive and enduring research into the realm of chemical manipulation is indeed an inquiry into the nature of photosensitive emulsion, both as pure matter and as a carrier of meaning. The alchemic idea of unity between mind and matter is expressed through this dual approach. The chemical process participates in the creation of meaning, while in reverse the photographic images are treated as pure matter. Remarkably, Reble uses a range of photographic toners in his filmmaking practice. Toning is a long-established photographic technique in which the metallic silver contained in the emulsion is swapped for other compounds such as copper (red), iron (blue), and even gold (sepia). In alchemy, metals are assumed to have interconnected relationships with particular parts of the earth, the body, physical health, and spiritual knowledge (see further Read, 1933). This is mirrored by Reble in his films and performances through an imaginative use of toners that underpins the expressiveness of the moving image. Furthermore, it is also relevant to mention that Reble studied physics – he did not attend art school, and his activities as an artist are primarily based on practical experience. Notably, he does not describe his films from a theoretical point of view but instead refers repeatedly to the process of making. In academia, such a practice-based approach is generally seen as ranking lower than theoretical knowledge. This hierarchy is also reflected in the arts, as evidenced in the frequent eulogising of conceptual approaches and a downgrading of craft-based methods. In Reble's work, 'knowledge is born from practice – another parallel with alchemic practice.

However, it is also important to draw out the differences between Reble's practice and alchemy. Pereira's insightful text discloses that by 'breaking the structure of material things, the alchemists thought they could turn concrete substances back into their original state of formless matter and then give it a new and more perfect form' (Pereira, 2000a: 118). Contrarily to this transhumanist-sounding project of the alchemists, Reble states that in his performance *Alchemie*, 'you observe a dance of the elements or a dance of atoms and molecules [...]. That is so dramatic to have that in forty minutes, and say; there will be nothing' (Doing, 2017: 116). To reiterate: in this performance, the spectator witnesses the formation and destruction of the moving image in real time through Reble's live chemical manipulation of a film loop. Reble's remark that in the end 'there will be nothing' expresses a materialist point of view referring to human culture in general and the moving image in particular. Seemingly, there is a contradiction in Reble's work between a 'cold' material observation of matter and a 'hot' spiritual signification. In order to understand this contradiction better, it is helpful to look at Thomas Köner's sonic contribution to both performances. As discussed, Köner uses contact microphones to pick up the sounds of the projector, the sizzling of the chemicals, and, in the performance *Tabula Smaragdina*, the sounds that are produced through the interaction of the heavily manipulated filmstrip and the optical sound-head of the projectors. Köner thus treats the projector and the film as 'objets sonore', sonorous objects, a term borrowed from the French composer Pierre Schaeffer:

The sonorous object, Schaeffer insisted, is not the instrument that produces it, not the medium in or on which it exists, and not the mind of the listener. Sounds are ontological particulars and individuals rather than qualities of objects or subjects. And this is why works of *musique concrète* are not representations – of objects in the world or of worldly sounds – but presentations of sonorous objects. (Cox, 2011: 156)

The difference between representation and presentation is key. The spectators find themselves 'inside' the projector and the chemical process, becoming aware of the visual and the sonic events instantaneously and synchronously. Cox modifies Schaeffer's concept by proposing that 'if sounds are particulars or individuals, then, they are so not as static *objects* but as temporal *events*' (ibid.). Furthermore, Cox elaborates this proposition by stating that 'sound is not a world apart, a unique domain of non-signification and non-representation. Rather, sound and the sonic arts are firmly rooted in the material world and the powers, forces, intensities, and becomings of which it is composed' (ibid., 157). The same argument can be applied to Reble's photochemical manipulations, which are as 'firmly rooted in the material world' as Köner's sonic explorations. Cox's argument relates to a broader direction in cultural studies that has become known as 'new materialism'.

New materialism is a broad field with several strands. What brings all of these researchers, writers, and practitioners together is a desire to move away from the prevailing anthropocentric worldview. From a classical humanist point of view, matter is regarded as inert and lacking agency. Within new materialism, different arguments are used to demonstrate that matter is more active than previously assumed. While new materialism is firmly based in the humanities, scientific insights are recurrently used to underpin their arguments. A good example can be found in the acclaimed book *Vibrant Matter: A Political Ecology of Things* by political theorist and philosopher Jane Bennett:

In a world of lively matter, we see that biochemical and biochemical-social systems can sometimes unexpectedly bifurcate or choose developmental paths that could not have been foreseen, for they are governed by an emergent rather than a linear or deterministic causality. And once we see this, we will need an alternative both to the idea of nature as a purposive, harmonious process and to the idea of nature as a blind mechanism. (Bennett, 2010: 112)

Bennett develops this idea by looking at diverse case studies such as the breakdown of the electric grid in North America in 2003, demonstrating that there is no single cause for a complex incident like this. Instead, a complex network of different actants, including politicians, squirrels, and electrons, all played their part. Subsequently, she seeks a new way of thinking that is more attuned to this broad congregation. This line of thought can be applied to material experiments in cinema as well. If we look again at *Tabula Smaragdina*, the significance of pulsating spheres, swarms of particles, forms that look like unicellular organisms, and sea creatures makes more sense. What we are witnessing is the formation of consciousness, emerging from a complex, always changing and moving pool of matter. From this point of view, Reble's spiritual approach and Jacobs's scientific approach can be brought together on the same plane. Both these filmmakers are investigating the material qualities of the cinematic apparatus, an investigation that is conjoined with a further inquiry into human perception and mind. The interaction between mind and material remains a highly contested subject, even between the different strands of new materialists. The fact that such conceptual understandings of mind and matter remain speculative opens the door to a variety of different interpretations. New materialism is often accused of being too vague and therefore open to spiritual or even mystical construals. The alchemic references in Reble's work suggest a similar connotation. However, the concrete complexity of photochemical matter in flux is treated as an intrinsically natural phenomenon, not a supernatural one. The spectators are placed within this process, experiencing the world, and their own thought process on a quantum level:

If we humans are performances of matter as much as anything else, then anything allegedly exceptional about us must be but a particular inflection of a fully generalizable behavior of nature. Thus, if humans speak, perhaps it is because nature already speaks, in countless proliferating languages, and therefore spoke us into existence. (Gamble, Hanan & Nail, 2019: 123)

In order to complete this inquiry into the relation between the praxis of alchemy and Reble's work, we need to examine the figure of the alchemist as well. In popular culture, alchemists are either presented as charlatans or as magicians. Such portrayals are nuanced by historians who draw a connection between the early discoveries made by alchemists and the later blossoming of chemistry as an exact science:

The craftsmen of that day who used chemical processes – the bleachers and dyers, the tanners, the makers of paint and varnish, the brewers, vintners, and distillers, the workers in metals and alloys, the glassmakers – inherited all the techniques and skills accumulated by the alchemists. (Haynes, 1952: 268)

However, the achievements of the alchemists were overshadowed by their unattainable ambition: 'Alchemy had become a cult, not mystical in its inspiration, but mysterious in its practices, with deliberate intent to deceive' (ibid.). The transition from alchemy to chemistry was also underpinned by the decline of visual discourse. As argued by art and science writer Adrian Holme, alchemical literature championed the integration between image and text: 'together they form a clear sequential narrative, amounting to a powerful visual argument, not merely a descriptive adjunct [to the text]' (Holme, 2014: 197). The genuine alchemist can therefore be described as a serious researcher, relying on experiential methods and communicating by means of visual discourse. Instead of strict objective observation as practised in science, alchemists would allow more subjective observations, investigating not only the properties but also the 'nature' of matter and process. In modern times, such a subjective approach is excluded from scientific research and relegated entirely to the domain of the arts. Not only Reble but many other artists have found inspiration in alchemy and the alchemists precisely because of this more open approach that includes subjectivity, favours practice over theory, and foregrounds visual discourse. Reble explicitly mentions the German painter, photographer, and filmmaker Sigmar Polke (1941–2010) as a source of inspiration. Film historian Thomas Elsaesser analyses Polke's methods in an article that looks at the connection between his paintings, photographs, and films:

One finds in his work examples of irradiation and solarization, of the dissolution or the afterlife of natural substances (fungus, rot, decay), of toxic chemicals and hallucinogenic drugs, of radioactivity, of granular textures and smooth powdery substances, as well as of the contrasting, but also complementary associations that link 'potatoes' and 'mushrooms' – two highly emblematic organisms in the Polke universe. (Elsaesser, 2019: 53)

The link between painting and filmmaking is a recurring theme within experimental film and does appear in a distinctive way in Reble's work. Particularly in his film *Instabile Materie* (1995), this connection is made concrete: 16mm filmstrips were developed, coloured with toners, and subsequently arranged on large glass plates, allowing a further sprinkling of chemicals. 'I worked like an abstract painter', he says, 'on these filmstrips, knowing that there will be interaction between these different layers, but not knowing what comes out finally' (Doing, 2017: 122). Instead of working frame by frame, the artist relied on bigger gestures, creating forms across frame lines and adjacent filmstrips. Such a reliance on chance and contingency 'marks a shift of cinema as a primarily visual medium [...] toward an idea of cinema as a medium of sensations rather than representations, of varied intensities and subtle but significant energies rather than either truth or illusion' (Elsaesser, 2019: 61).

New materialism also applies to these films from a film historical perspective. In his book *Materialist Film*, filmmaker and writer Peter Gidal revisits and expands the theory of structural/materialist filmmaking that he developed in the 1970s. Gidal writes: 'Film-works can produce an analytic situation in the very processes of their procedure, not as an academic afterthought, not as analysis *versus* film-as-projected' (Gidal 1989: 8). The aim of this approach is not only to formulate a broad and incisive critique of the cinematic apparatus but also to engage the spectator actively in the construction of meaning. A warning against a too-literal interpretation of process-oriented cinema appears as well:

The fetishization of process, related to involvement with the 16 mm Co-op developing and printing equipment, became a major detour for some structural/materialist film, largely via the misappropriation of a materialist aesthetic to a positivist reading of the filmic apparatus. (Ibid., 35)

When judged on their formal qualities, the films of Reble have much in common with the structural/materialist films made in the 1970s. But his work also differs from them significantly when approached from a semiotic perspective. Rather than aiming to 'produce an analytic situation', Reble is involved in a 'positivist reading of the filmic apparatus' by deliberately and extensively using the illusionistic power at hand. But instead of this being merely fetishistic, his films and performances confront the viewer with a spectacle that is simultaneously highly engaging and intellectually challenging. The term 'new materialism' acquires a double meaning within this context, relating both to a contemporary approach of foregrounding the material qualities of film and to Bennett's 'lively matter' or Barad's 'agential realism' (further discussed in chapter 9). Modern insights such as relativity theory and quantum mechanics have re-enchanted science by introducing an element of doubt into physics. The Nobel Prize–winning theoretical physicist Werner Heisenberg wrote in 1962:

Any concepts or words which have been formed in the past through the interplay between the world and ourselves are not really sharply defined with respect to their meaning, that is to say, we don't know exactly how far they will help us in finding our way in the world. We often know that they can be applied to a wide range of inner or outer experience, but we practically never know precisely the limits of their applicability. This is true even of the most general concepts like 'existence' and 'space and time'. Therefore, it will never be possible by pure reason to arrive at some absolute truth. (Heisenberg, 2000: 51)

As Heisenberg predicted, this realisation has had a profound impact that has resonated beyond physics and found its way into philosophy and the arts. The films and expanded cinema performances of Jürgen Reble demonstrate this coming together of two seemingly opposed worldviews in a unique way. Reble has succeeded in bringing together his interest in physics and his fascination with alchemy by enticing the spectator to think about how the image came about, both in a purely material and detached way and in an incorporeal and speculative way. It is precisely the tension between a reductionist and a holistic point of view that makes his work so powerful and thought-provoking.

5

Eat Sleep Film Repeat

In 1994, I was invited to take part in an event in Paradiso, a legendary cultural centre in the heart of Amsterdam. I found myself among several dozen cultural entrepreneurs who presented their ideas. The event was organised by *Blvd.*, a lifestyle magazine that billed itself as a platform for a new generation bringing together art, film, fashion, and technology. Head shots of the participants captioned with short quotes appeared in their magazine alongside articles about Douglas Coupland, graffiti T-shirts, and information overload (van der Zande, 1994). Among the invited start-ups was XS4ALL, one of the first Dutch internet service providers. They were handing out floppy disks containing basic software for internet access and email to all the participants. The company was already growing at a fast rate, but at the time many people, including myself, did not yet realise the enormous impact that this technology would have on society. However, the trailblazers of the internet foresaw a fast-emerging cyber utopia as exemplified by the following zealous vision published by an American market-oriented think tank: 'Cyberspace is the land of knowledge, and the exploration of that land can be a civilization's truest, highest calling. The opportunity is now before us to empower every person to pursue that calling in his or her own way' (Dyson et al., 1994). This new contagious utopianism quickly spread around the globe, supercharged by further innovations in technology and media. A noteworthy contributor to this newly found belief in technological progress was the introduction of digital video (DV) by a consortium of video camera manufacturers in 1995. This new format came in various sizes, including the mini-DV format, which quickly became popular among independent filmmakers and artists. These technological innovations marked the advent of the digital era and simultaneously incentivised a change in perspective on what was now seen as 'old media'. Concurrently, the 100th anniversary of the birth of cinema was being widely celebrated, with the shooting of *L'arrivée d'un Train en Gare de La Ciotat* in 1895 and the subsequent first public film projection in 1896 by the Lumière Brothers considered as the pivotal moment when film was 'invented'. A large number of public screenings, TV broadcasts, exhibitions, and publications firmly established the perception of analog film as a historical medium. In the years running up to this landmark event, film archives in multiple countries had begun to call for action to preserve quickly deteriorating cinematic heritage for future generations. Their initial focus was directed toward the silent-film era and the notorious highly flammable nitrate-based films that were produced during that period. Many of these films had started to deteriorate, and there were no copies available to replace them. The Dutch Filmmuseum was at the forefront of this rescue effort, deciding that a new public-facing approach would be a key factor for rallying further support. The museum redoubled their efforts to bring pioneering film productions back onto the screen. Archivist Peter Delpeut proposed that instead of simply preserving the films and filing each title in a static archive, it would be useful to create an entirely new film that would not only showcase the original material but also provide a contemporary context. Delpeut focused on the archive of Jean Desmet, a Dutch film pioneer and entrepreneur who had collected more than 900 film prints from across the world. This unique collection of nitrate films, including tinted, toned, and hand-coloured prints, had been transferred to the Dutch Filmmuseum in 1957, a year after Desmet's death. The preservation of this fragile collection would take several decades, as such an extensive project was unprecedented within the archive. Delpeut took advantage of the partial deterioration of the film material and integrated footage heavily marked by decay in his film *Lyrical Nitrate* (1991). Instead of framing the footage within a traditional narrative, the film approaches the collection as a set of images that refer to the medium itself. The film opens with a sequence of shots that refer to optical instruments such as binoculars and microscopes. Subsequently, a scene set inside a cinema follows. Remarkably, this scene not only focuses on the film's projection but also on the audience, the owner, and the projectionist. Next, a series of urban scenes places the cinema within the broader context of the meteoric rise of modernity during the first decades of the twentieth century by highlighting fast-moving transport such as trams, trains, and steamships. After this opening, a series of scenes follow that not only show the beauty and continuing appeal of silent cinema but also capture the rapidly changing relationships between genders and cultural frameworks. Modern concepts such as feminism, gender fluidity, and multiculturalism are only a stone's throw away. The film concludes with a sequence of increasingly deteriorated images in which the representational aspect of film is overtaken, step by step, by its material transience. As noted by film scholar André Habib, the film goes beyond a historical narrative through its use of fragments:

Refusing the imperatives of positive history (analyzing, dating, understanding, informing), but without succumbing to pure, formal play (looping, abstract or associative montage), Delpeut tries to present an allegory of cinema, a lyrical art, discontinuous and fragmented. Even more, he turns the discontinued and fragmented state of the rediscovered nitrate into the very source of cinema's lyricism. (Habib, 2006: 131)

Furthermore Habib comments on the deteriorated images as being a 'live imprint of exposed time, which continues to corrode itself following the same time pattern as human time, precisely because it participates in the same temporality as human time – one oriented towards finitude' (ibid., 135). *Lyrical Nitrate* touches upon several issues that were thrown into stark relief within the context of the emerging digital era: the vulnerable status of the moving image, the profound impact of technological change, and the resulting remodelling of human relationships. However, instead of addressing such issues in a narrative or expository way, the film rather presents the spectator with an archive in flux, destabilising notions of permanence and fixed historicity. Delpeut's film is vital, both in terms of reinterpretation of the original footage and because it foregrounds the instability of the nitrate material that has been altered by fungal growth.

This focus on the archive and the construction of new meaning is also at the heart of Vincent Monnikendam's film *Mother Dao, the Turtlelike* (1995). This film is based on footage produced by, and in support of, Dutch colonialists. The original footage either showcases the efficiency of the various plantations and enterprises in the Dutch Indies, celebrates the lifestyle of the colonialists, or sings the praise of their 'civilising' activities such as public health initiatives. Monnikendam upends these objectives through a reversal of the gaze, placing the people subjected to the oppressive Dutch regime at the centre in his associative and at times surreal montage. The film opens with a shot of a child whose amenable gaze changes into bashfulness in a few seconds (see figure 5.1). The spectator is immediately put into the role of voyeur while also lowering their guard due to the loveable appearance of the child. After the main title, a series of slow-motion images of a violent volcanic eruption stir up a completely different feeling. A voice starts speaking in Indonesian, narrating an otherworldly creation myth that elucidates the title of the film. Images of people living in what seem to be precolonial circumstances underline this mythical parable. After this opening, the film cuts to scenes set in factories, mines, and fields where people toil relentlessly. Instead of focusing on the great achievements of the colonialists, the spectator's attention is turned toward the predicament of the local workers. As noted by film scholar Fatimah Tobing Rony:

We are looking at the eyes of those who are condemned to eternal hell. The horror slowly dawns that this is a world in which humans are the slaves of a nightmarish assortment of machines, factories, plantations, and mines that use human bodies as their fuel. The life moments of birth, marriage and death – so beloved by anthropologists and travelogues – take on a new meaning. (Rony, 2003: 150–151)

Figure 5.1 *Mother Dao, the Turtlelike* – Vincent Monnikendam (NL 1995, 35mm film, bw, 90 minutes); courtesy of the artist.

The repressive gaze of the original films is effectively reversed by Monikkendam. However, the resulting narrative is not presented in a linear form but in an associative complex arrangement of interconnected situations in which the social relationship between the oppressors and their subjects are deconstructed in full view of the spectator. An important role is allotted to the soundtrack, which consists of a mix of noises, musical elements, and the voice-over. Together, these elements create a dreamlike atmosphere, as if the cinematic experience is brought to us by the restless spirits of the people who were subjected to limitless greed and cruelty.

The renewed interest in the archive, materiality, and untold or repressed stories was certainly not confined to the Netherlands. Bill Morisson, a young artist who had attended Robert Breer's animation classes at Cooper Union in downtown New York, became involved with the Ridge Theater in Manhattan, where he met a number of musicians involved in the new music scene, such as Bill Frisell. Morisson started working with archive footage inspired by groundbreaking filmmakers such as Joseph Cornell and Bruce Conner, and more recently by Peter Delpeut and his *Lyrical Nitrate*. Initially, his films were made to be projected on stage, embedded in the company's theatre productions. In 1996, he made *The Film of Her*, a twelve-minute film that was widely shown at both archival and experimental film gatherings and festivals. Like *Lyrical Nitrate* and *Mother Dao*, Morisson's film starts with a reference to cinema, in this case a shot of a hand taking a film can from a shelf lined with similar cans. Like the opening sequence in Delpeut's film, Morisson also draws parallels between technological advances and the rapid expansion of the cinematic medium. A lens is shifted in front of a candle, indicating the beginning of a cinema show. This is followed by a sequence of shots relating to scientific advances and industrialisation. Notably, both are visualised with the aid of precision optics and time-lapse photography. The scene ends with a machine that perforates 35mm film. After the main title, a rapidly edited sequence shows trees being felled, chopped into logs and pulped, producing boards and paper. Again, this refers back to cinema by linking the production of paper to the production of paper prints, a medium that was used for copyright purposes during the early years of cinema. A huge collection of paper prints was stored at the Library of Congress, discovered by a clerk who realised the significance of this collection only moments before the prints were due to be incinerated. In an interview with film scholar Scott MacDonald, who is well-known for publishing interviews with independent and experimental filmmakers, Bill Morisson elaborates:

Because the paper print rolls were finally preserved, the earliest films have lasted decades longer than many films produced after them – original nitrate negatives were incredibly flammable, combustible, easily lost in warehouse fires. We have a relatively complete history of cinema from 1896 to 1912, whereas what we have preserved from 1912 to 1948, the remaining years of nitrate film production, is relatively scant. (MacDonald, 2016: 125)

The Film of Her recounts these relatively unknown facts in an imaginative way. The selected archive footage is edited in a style reminiscent of the dialectic approach of early Soviet cinema: it visually constructs a chain of events like the felling of trees in a forest and the subsequent industrial production of paper prints. Instead of slow motion, an effect that is used in both *Lyrical Nitrate* and *Mother Dao,* Morisson chooses fast motion, inspired by his own experience of living in a fast-paced city. A second remarkable element is the weaving in of an early stag film, showing a naked woman who smiles seductively at the camera before and after apparently having intercourse with a fugitive male character. Her appearance is presented as the motivation that drove the clerk to prevent the destruction of the paper prints. The clerk is not only in love with cinema but also personifies the cinephile for whom the star that appears on the silver screen is 'larger than life'. Hence, the spectator is drawn into the Freudian depth of their own relationship with the screen. Analogous to the hidden transience of film's materiality, which is brought out in *Lyrical Nitrate,* and repressed postcolonial culpability, which resurfaces in *Mother Dao, The Film of Her* brings out a restrained sexual desire concealed within the history of cinema.

Sexuality and gender are also central themes in a trilogy made by the Austrian experimental filmmaker Martin Arnold: *Pièce Touchée* (1989), *Passage a l'Acte* (1993), and *Alone, Life Wastes Andy Hardy* (1998). Arnold uses seemingly trivial scenes from Hollywood films, reworking these on an optical printer. *Pièce Touchée* is situated in a room where a woman is waiting for her husband, who comes back after doing an important job (see figure 5.2). *Passage a l'Acte* focuses on a family at the dinner table, and *Alone, Life Wastes Andy Hardy* features a scene in which a son affirms his love for both his mother and his girlfriend while he rejects his father's authority. Each of these extracts illustrates the outmoded gender

Figure 5.2 *Pièce Touchée* – Martin Arnold (AT 1989, 16mm film, bw, 15min); courtesy of the artist.

roles typical of much of Hollywood's output throughout its first hundred years. Through the process of rephotographing small sections, while the original footage is forwarded and reversed, new gestures, expressions, and meanings are created. The actors repeat the same partial movements again and again, caught in an agonising stutter. As the timeframe slowly shifts, their faltering gestures continuously change, but each change is so small that it is hard to perceive the discrete steps individually. The result is an astonishing cinematic spectacle that creeps under the skin of the spectator in a way that is simultaneously unsettling and exciting. In an interview with Scott MacDonald, the artist talks about this aspect of his work:

Many people experience *Pièce Touchée* as very erotic; I've been asked again and again why it's so sexual. I think that this impression originates on a formal level, as the product of that irregular vibration. The representation of genders adds to this and channels this instinctive mood. In the beginning I was surprised myself about the multiplicity of possible ways to influence meaning. (MacDonald, 1998: 352)

He further elaborates on the significance of such formal aspects: 'Forms, colors, contrast, and rhythms don't affect the spectator in the realm of language and logic; they communicate on deeper levels: I would situate the discourse they take part in in the unconscious' (ibid.). This realm beyond language is something that is missing from standard archival practice, where the task of the archivist is usually understood as the unaltered preservation and restoration of the original. Notably, not only is the image drastically reorganised in *Passage a l'Acte* and *Alone, Life Wastes Andy Hardy*, but so is the sound. By playing, reversing, and repeating snippets of the original sound, a scratch, hip-hop, and electronic music–related track is created that draws the footage into a contemporary realm that is neither fully digital nor fully analog in its appearance. This is notwithstanding the fact that the films are made on an optical printer and primarily projected on 16mm, a connection with the new aesthetic possibilities of digital processing surfaces. While repetition has long been explored in experimental film, exemplified by classic experimental films such as Peter Kubelka's *Schwechater* (1958) and David Rimmer's *Variations on a Cellophane Wrapper* (1972), the emergence of the digital sampler and the animated GIF have brought repetitive sound and motion into popular culture. Sampled drum sounds are widely used but also concrete noise, and sampled voices have become much more commonplace in a variety of musical genres. Animated GIFs became known early on as a solution for the integration of moving images on the web but have remained popular until the present. This format has popularised the use of short looped animations of the human body in motion. Arnold's optical printing technique connects the formal explorations of structural filmmaking with these new, now common, digital deformations of sound and moving image. Moreover, it is important to point out that the sensual and erotic experience that Arnold's films offer is not an easy one. His films do not provide an escapist illusion but rather present the characters as automatons driven by a set of cultural codes and sexual instincts. Film and media scholar David Bering-Porter comments on the strangeness of the spectator's experience:

What is unsettling about Arnold's films is the way they reflect the uncanniness within our own movements, our own bodies, and are suggestive of alien or unconscious motivations behind our gestures. They intimate that, somewhere, there is an automaton in all of us. (Bering-Porter, 2014: 182)

In the expanded cinema performances I made in collaboration with sound artist Pierre Bastien, repetitions, loops, and automatons also took on an important role. Rather than a mechanisation of the body, our departure point was a humanisation of the machine. Bastien is widely known for playing with a home-built mechanical music orchestra. When we started working together, he was performing with an orchestra of Meccano-based mechanisms driven by pickup motors. These rough and ready robots could produce rhythms by hitting drums and plucking or bowing string instruments. Bastien was using a mix of African, Asian, and European instruments, bringing together the sounds of world music and the rhythms of electronic music. During live performances, shadows of this hybrid orchestra were projected, while obscuring the audience's view of the multi-instrumentalist himself, who not only operated the machines but also played solos on a pocket trumpet. For our joint performance, we made a series of Super 8 and 16mm films that featured his musical machines in a rhythmical montage intercut with pulsating animations and undulating forms. Bastien made a new series of machines, not playing musical instruments anymore, but tools and everyday objects like pliers, scissors, a saw, and a letter scale. The films were projected in alternating single-, double-, and triple-screen format, intermittently accompanied by shadow projections of Bastien's musical machines. These shadows were created with a handheld torch (see figure 5.3). The composition of both sound and image was based on loops, spinning and repetitive patterns, and reverse or palindromic constructions. Besides the repetitive and mechanical element, there was an element of contingency. The machines and the projectors would never play at the exact same speed, and the starting and stopping of multiple devices was done manually. The result was a pattern of subtly shifting rhythms that appeared more human than machine-like. Although we did not use any archival footage in *Rotary Factory* (1996), our first collaboration, the effect was a kind of alternate future in which state-of-the-art digital looping and sampling are brought back into the realm of pre-digital devices. Grainy black-and-white footage, rattling projectors, and Bastien's melancholic melodies all added to this mood of technological reversal, while the musical machines contributed a surreal element. Bastien's work is indebted to Raymond Roussel, an eccentric poet admired by the Surrealists. In his experimental novel

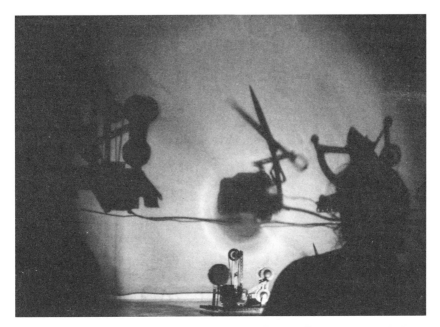

Figure 5.3 *Rotary Factory* – Pierre Bastien & Karel Doing (NL 1996, expanded cinema performance, 30min).

Impressions of Africa, Roussel meticulously describes a gala in honour of the emperor Talu VII. A series of bewildering acts and experiments are performed in front of the royal family and the assembled crowd, ranging from a fencing match to a zither-playing worm. Many of these acts are accompanied by perplexing mechanisms which are described in much detail. The inventor Bedu demonstrates a miraculous loom that brings to mind the famous Jacquard machine, a precursor of the programmable computer:

The paddles underneath drove the whole machine without any assistance, by means of their own complex and precise action – some of them remaining immersed almost continuously, while others were only dipped in the current for a few seconds at a time; several of the smallest only brushed the water with their blades for a moment and quickly rose again, dropping back in the same fleeting manner after a brief pause. Their number, their graduated sizes, the way they plunged into the water, separately or together, briefly or for a longer period, all these factors provided an endless variety of combinations, favouring the execution of the boldest designs. One might have mistaken it for some silent musical instrument, striking cords or playing arpeggios, some simple, others extremely intricate, whose rhythm and harmony were constantly recurring. (Roussel, 2011: 70-71)

Just like Roussel's mechanisms, Bastien's machines are not merely functional. Due to their fascinating appearance and surprising musicality Bastien's contraptions take on the role of performers. The film loops and shadow projections bring a visual element to this ingenuous sonic universe, providing a more intimate encounter with these captivating machines. Bastien makes sure that the audience's attention is fully focused on his mechanical orchestra by concealing himself in semi-darkness. The ensuing rhythms and melodies are reminiscent of drum machines and sequencers, but instead of being produced by electronic devices, the music is 'played' by automatons assembled by the artist, from pickup motors and Meccano construction elements.

In our next expanded cinema performance titled *Recollection* (1998), we did use archival footage, not by working with an actual film archive but by picking up discarded corporate films, documentaries, and propaganda films from street markets. I started working with this footage by isolating human gestures and circular movements of vehicles, objects, and tools. I used the contact printer at Studio één to print this footage repeatedly, which gave me the opportunity to create repetitive movements and erase the original corporate agenda contained in the found footage. Instead of echoing an optimistic modernist ideology, the reworked version brings me back to the title of this chapter, an internet meme that has been boosted into popularity by 'Eat Sleep Rave Repeat' (2013), a track by Fatboy Slim, Riva Star, and Beardyman. The lyrics of this song evoke a world full of violence and drug abuse in which raving is the only escape. Instead of repetition being pointless, the repetitive music and accompanying dance movements induce a soothing trance. Similarly, the workers and objects in *Recollection* repeat their (semi-)circular movements and gestures without ever going forward. But instead of this being futile and depressing, a surreal form of dance emerges which would not be misplaced at a rave. Again, the films were projected in a multi-screen format with movements coinciding and diverging like syncopated rhythms. Bastien designed a mechanism that allowed him to play short sections of a selection of vintage records. The needle of his prepared record player was lifted and dropped mechanically, playing the same groove repetitively. The imperfection of his system resulted in unpredictable variations within a small margin. The effect was that a certain section would repeat numerous times, before jumping to an almost identical section at a given moment. Similarly to the association between old and new technology kindled by Arnold's films, this mechanised and repetitive music operated somewhere between scratch, jazz, electronic, and ethnic music. While Arnold's repetitive sequences express an uneasy ambivalence between erotic impulses and neurotic tics, the repetitions in our expanded cinema performance resulted in a more hypnotic and forlorn tone. Machines and humans seemed to be implicated in the same situation, repeating faltering movements, gestures, and sounds without ever taking a clear path forward. Instead of connecting humans and machines in a narrative about jubilant technological progress, our protagonists appeared aimless and imperfect, albeit in a pleasantly melancholic and contemplative way.

In their film *Dervish Machine* (1992), Jeanne Liotta and Bradley Eros also use repetition to create a particular experience. The title refers to the famous Sufi dance ritual that 'is a special way of training the dervish's perception and awareness; it is a kind of meditation where consciousness can penetrate the metaphysical world' (Erzen, 2008) while simultaneously paraphrasing Brion Gysin's *Dreamachine* (1960):

a cardboard cylinder with holes on a fixed distance that was placed on a 78 rpm turntable with a light bulb within. When the turntable starts spinning the light will come out with a regular frequency within the 8–12 Hz alpha range, similar to a laboratory stroboscope. (ter Meulen, Tavy & Jacobs, 2009: 318–319).

The purpose of this device is to induce a 'drugless high', comparable with the elevated state of awareness of the dancing dervish. However, the machine produces this effect in an effortless way that does not require long training. In *Dervish Machine*, rotating objects, whirling bodies, and flickering light are linked not only to the concept of heightened awareness but also to the transient nature of life. The film was made during the height of the AIDS crisis, when thousands of young men and women were dying after being infected by the virus. A naked woman and a skeleton embrace each other in a circular dance; while standing on a gravestone, her body is elevated into the air. An angel-like figure dances on top of a platform while her body is engulfed in a flood of light. Images of a rotting corpse in a coffin are intercut with a dancing figure wearing a strange death mask. All of this is shot on Super 8 and hand-developed impromptu, producing stains, scratches, colour effects, and other imperfections on the emulsion. The image sometimes flips backward and forward between negative and positive, similar to the technique that is used by Michael Brynntrup in his film *Totentanz 8* (see chapter 1). Taken together, the moving, rotating, and flickering images bring the spectator into a dreamlike state, enhanced by the fleetingness of faces, bodies, objects, and text. Some images appear only during one, two or three frames, registering merely at the edge of conscious perception. The soundtrack is composed of snippets of baroque music which are repeated and deformed. This deformation is achieved by playing scratchy records on a loop and by gradually slowing down magnetic tape. The fragile materiality of the film's emulsion is brought together with the similarly fugitive materiality of vinyl records and reel-to-reel tapes. Through the synchronisation of these normally unwanted deformations in sound and image, a subversive logic emerges. Instead of presenting an escapist reality, *Dervish Machine* invites the spectator to explore the boundaries between the temporal and the eternal. The recurring spinning movement cuts across machine and body, uniting the automated object and the organic body in a never-ending dance.

In this last example, a minimal amount of archival footage appears, but the reference to, and appearance of, the Dreamachine certainly functions within this work as a form of technological reversal or media archaeology. This is not a simple nostalgic repetition of the past but a creative reworking of aesthetics and technology from the (recent) past into an artwork that is finely attuned to its zeitgeist. In turn, the Dreamachine can be placed in a longer history of mechanical devices and optical illusions and the psychological effects that these might create. In her groundbreaking book *The Optical Unconscious*, art historian Rosalind Krauss describes the experience produced by Marcel Duchamp's *Rotary Demisphere (Precision Optics)* (1925):

First there is the disk as eye; then it appears as breast; this then gives way to the fictive presence of a uterine cavity and the implication of sexual penetration. And within this pulse, as it carries one from part-object to part-object, advancing and receding through the illusion of three dimensional space, there is also a hint of the persecutory threat that the object poses for the viewer, a threat carried by the very metamorphic rhythm itself, as its constant thrusting of the form into a state of dissolve brings on the experience of formlessness, seeming to overwhelm the once-bounded object with the condition of the *informe*. (Krauss, 1994: 137)

This connection between the eye, the pulsating machine, and the induction of an ambiguous erotic experience is also present in *Dervish Machine* with its whirling and flickering movements and glimpses of naked bodies that appear in conjunction with traces of death and decay. As opposed to the structural films from the 1960s and 1970s, which were aimed at the deconstruction of cinematic illusion, Liotta and Eros rather confront the viewer with a spectacle that freely uses both formal and symbolic elements. In the opening sequence of the film, the shadow of a rotating film reel appears. A pan to the left reveals a young man standing next to a 16mm film projector. The camera zooms in on the lens of the projector until the screen is filled with a circle of white light, turning the projector into an illuminated eye that looks back at us.

The tumultuous arrival of the digital era and the historicisation of cinema overwhelmingly confirmed the notion that analog film was an outmoded and redundant medium. However, the above examples substantiate a more complex chronicle, subverting the idea of linear progress. Filmmakers such as Delpeut, Monnikendam, and Morisson have shown that revisiting and reworking historical footage can lead to astonishing results which bring out formerly ignored connotations already present in the original material. It should not come as a surprise that these filmmakers include the specific history of the cinematic apparatus and the broader history of seeing within their work. Delpeut does this explicitly by taking us into a silent movie theatre, Monnikendam reverses the colonial gaze by putting the enslaved people centre stage, and Morisson takes us into an almost forgotten and destroyed archive that comes back to life before our very eyes. Beyond this sophisticated reworking of 'found footage', the subsequent examples confirm a further fruitful experimentation with looping, sampling, and scratching (the turntablist technique). Arnold's precise elongations of mundane scenes gleaned from mainstream Hollywood cinema cast a new light on the compulsive behavioural patterns in which the protagonists are trapped. The sonic and optical loops, spinning and repetitive patterns that are produced by projector, torch, and musical mechanism in the expanded cinema performances by me and Pierre

Bastien create a hypnotic parallel world in which rotating objects and bodies extend their life beyond utilitarianism. Finally, Liotta and Eros's *Dervish Machine* balances somewhere between erotic dream and existential nightmare by exploiting flicker and rotation in conjunction with a bold new form of symbolism. These imaginative works of experimental cinema demonstrate that standard archival practice is a procedure that only preserves a fraction of the richness of cinema's history. Fortunately, experimental filmmakers are well positioned to make up for this institutional gap. The next chapter will show how this development has swept around the globe and dig deeper into notions of destruction and disappearance – topics that have become increasingly important due to the multiplication of global crises like global heating, radioactive contamination, corporate greed, media monopolisation, and the decline of democratic values.

6

Rebirth

The artist-run lab movement grew steadily, with more and more independent labs opening their doors. Several long-running labs expanded their scope and acquired more professional equipment. The new opportunities offered by the internet and email contributed to this development and were exploited by the community as a space to exchange, share, and store knowledge about experimental and independent cinema production, distribution, and exhibition. The community grew into a network of partners, including not only collectively run labs but also small commercial enterprises, archives, and universities. Not only did the artist-run film labs interact with these partners, but in many cases these hybrid organisations also took over parts of the activities that were formerly the exclusive domain of industry and institutions. After moving from Arnhem to Rotterdam, my own initiative, Studio één, went through a period of accelerated expansion due to an increasing demand for Super 8 services. Simultaneously, with access to new funding possibilities and other kinds of institutional support, it became possible to expand the lab's artistic activities as well. This dual nature eventually led to the lab splitting into two quite different structures: a new collective named Filmwerkplaats (Film Workshop) and a new company called Super 8 Reversal Lab. Both are still contributing to the wider experimental film community. The Super 8 Reversal Lab caters to a wide range of professionals and amateurs who work with small-gauge film formats and obsolete photographic materials for a variety of reasons. The company, run by Frank Bruinsma, has grown into a well-oiled service provider while maintaining a passionate relationship to cinema culture. Simultaneously, the Filmwerkplaats has grown into a formidable centre for handmade film, including facilities for developing, editing, printing, and projection. Founding member Esther Urlus has undertaken multiple projects into 'the creation, preservation and circulation of technical knowledge of analogue film in order to support its use as a creative medium' (Re-Engineering the Moving Image, 2016). One of these projects is focused on handmade emulsion making, reviving early photochemical experiments. One of the outcomes of this project is Urlus's film *Konrad & Kurfurst* (2014), in which she foregrounds the painterly effect engendered by handmade emulsion. The film is presented as a re-enactment of a crash that took place during the 1936 Olympic Games in Berlin involving the horse Kürfurst and its rider, Konrad von Wangenheim. From a tempest of particles and air bubbles, the image of a swimming horse briefly becomes visible, transforming its quotidian appearance into a cosmic entity, forming and disintegrating in and out of pure materiality. Urlus has published her research into handmade emulsion making in a self-published guide that provides lists of ingredients and step-by-step instructions for the aspiring filmmaker (Urlus, 2013). This project goes well beyond the activities of a traditional film archive by focussing on the continuation of knowledge rather than the preservation of artefacts. A second example of such an 'anarchival' approach is the Charter of Cinematographic Projection in the 21st Century, an initiative undertaken by Nicholas Rey, one of the founding members of l'Abominable in Paris. The charter highlights the critical situation of the projection of film prints, a medium that has been almost entirely replaced by digital projection. The signatories question this development and seek to work toward a more balanced situation in which both film projection equipment and knowledge concerning the specifics of projecting photochemical motion picture prints are preserved for future generations. L'Abominable has grown into a well-equipped film laboratory that includes black-and-white and colour processing machines, telecine, subtitling, and many other facilities. The lab is run collectively and regularly organises screenings and events. A 300-page catalogue of films made in the lab can be downloaded from their website (l'Abominable, 2022). At present, the lab is moving its entire operation to a new location, a cultural district that is in the process of development and will be housed in the former Éclair film laboratory. The collective has also adopted a new name: Navire Argo. The name is derived from the mythical ship that carried the Argonauts during their quest to find the Golden Fleece. On their new website, the ambition to propel photochemical cinema into a new direction is clarified:

Filmmakers will now pick up where these technicians left off, opening the doors of the screening room to the public. The very industry that remained inaccessible to many filmmakers will now be put to the service of contemporary photochemical film practices and the perpetuation of hands-on skills and technical knowledge. (Navire Argo, 2022)

Many smaller artist-run labs operate with a similar agenda in mind, putting the filmmaker in charge of the technical means of production. As argued, the benefit of this approach is greater artistic freedom. But it is also increasingly clear that the task of safeguarding the future of photochemical film as an artistic medium is not an easy one. The artist-run labs network has spread beyond the countries which already have a long-standing infrastructure that allows the safeguarding of cinema culture through institutional programs of collection and preservation. This is important in the context of a much-broader struggle in the field of film history and theory against cultural hegemony by dominant nation-states such as the founding members of the International Federation of Film Archives (FIAF): France, the UK, Germany, and the US (see further Wood, 2010). New independent artist-run labs have been established in countries like Indonesia, Mexico, the Baltic states, and numerous others. The following examples will demonstrate the significance of this new direction.

In 2016, the Baltic Analog Lab was founded in Riga, Latvia. The collective runs a workspace, organises an experimental film festival, and runs a program of workshops and events. One of these events focused on amateur filmmaking in the Latvian Soviet Socialist Republic, presenting two programmes of previously almost completely overlooked experimental films made in the period between the 1970s and 90s. During communism, film production was highly regulated by the state, and experimental film was certainly not pursued by the authorities as a desirable direction. However, throughout the Soviet Union, amateur film clubs were sponsored by the state and thriving. An article in *Culture Crossroads*, a journal published by the Latvian Academy of Culture, explains how these clubs could develop into a platform for experimentation:

Socialist ideology was pushing amateur filmmaking out of the home and trying to encourage its social uses. At the same time, through various control mechanisms that were an inevitable component of state funding, its use for oppositional purposes was also limited. However, since amateur cinema in the Soviet Union had minimal distribution, no centralized governmental body existed to control and censor the output of amateur filmmaking clubs, in contrast to the professional film industry. (Strupele, 2017: 64)

The Baltic Analog Lab has taken the initiative to save and collect these forgotten experimental films, often in close contact with the filmmakers or their relatives. In collaboration with the Latvian State Archive, some of the films were digitalised and made publicly available online. Two screenings were organised to bring a broader selection of these films back on the screen (in their original format). An impressive example is the film *Mijkrēšļa rotaļa ar spoguli / Twilight Play with a Mirror* (1972) by Ivars Skanstiņš. This fifteen-minute film is part of a series of short films made by the members of the experimental theatre group Birojs in which each member gave their point of view on society. Only two films out of this series have survived the suppression of the Soviet secret police, the notorious KGB. Arguably, because of its ambiguous and playful nature Skanstiņš's film was left untouched and got screened at festivals. The members of the Birojs group appear in the film, performing partially improvised actions in a public space with an empty picture frame, a mirror, a milk bottle, and an 8mm camera (see figure 6.1). The frame is used alternately to present the performers as individuals or as a group, the mirror to reflect either group

Figure 6.1 *Mijkrēšļa Rotaļa ar Spoguli / Twilight Play with a Mirror* – Ivars Skanstiņš (LV 1972, 16mm film, bw, 15min); courtesy of Baltic Analog Lab.

members or parts of the (urban) landscape, while the milk bottle is passed around in a performative manner. The 8mm camera reinforces the notion of self-reflexivity that runs through the film, placing the film firmly within a much-broader movement of self-conscious art that aims to comment on the process of its own making. It is remarkable that the film fits seamlessly into a wider trend while simultaneously being entirely authentic and original. As such, this film and its contemporaries deserve further study that could lead to a reconsideration of the history of experimental film as a primarily Western European and North American tradition.

A further example is the Mexican artist-led initiative Laboratorio Experimental de Cine (LEC), which was founded in 2013 by Morris Trujilo and Elena Pardo. LEC has organised many film screenings, expanded cinema events, and workshops. In 2017, LEC submitted a proposal to Churubusco, the oldest film studio in Mexico. This state-run studio includes a lab that used to work nonstop but is not so busy anymore. Trujilo and Pardo invited a group of filmmakers to make a film about the laboratory, involving its union workers. The end of the project was marked by an international artist-run film labs meeting, which was attended by 130 people from around the world, making visible the liveliness of experimental film culture in Mexico. Another noteworthy collaborative work began during an archivist meeting in Oaxaca, where Pardo met with Inti Garcia, a teacher from Huautla Jiménez, a community in the Mazatec region of Oaxaca. In an interview with media conservator Walter Forsberg, she provides a short account of this project:

Inti's family ran a movie theatre and made screenings in remote communities, carrying 35mm projectors on their backs. Renato García Dorantes, Inti's father, learned how to use a video camera and started making his own documentary films. When Renato died, Inti inherited a vast film collection and dreamed of building a community center where people can have access to these materials, and can learn about traditional architecture, cooking, mushroom culture, and the whistling language. (Forsberg, 2021: 100)

Pardo co-directed a short film together with a local filmmaker, Tzutzu Matzin, who had worked on the digitisation of the archive. This film, which is titled *Cinema'a o de Cómo Curar el Mal de Archivo* (2016), combines documentary footage with animation and archival images. Through this hybridity, the film shows the relationship between traditional arts and culture, the film and video archive, the collection of cameras, projectors, and recorders, and the dream of establishing a community centre. Similar to the plight of many indigenous communities, Mazatec culture is in decline. Pardo and Matzin's film aims to raise awareness of the fight against further erosion of this unique culture by showing the interrelatedness of cultural activities, artefacts (such as films and videos), and tools (including 16mm and 35mm cameras and projectors). Inti's collection thus represents a body of knowledge that only remains alive through an interdisciplinary form of practice that transcends the focus of a traditional museum or archive.

In this light, it is also relevant to look at the temporary occupation of the Indonesian State Production Film Centre (PFN) by a group of artists operating under the name Lab Laba Laba (Spider Lab). When the acclaimed Indonesian film director Edwin was looking for a film splicer, he discovered the neglected archive of the PFN. More than 800 titles were left in a storage room without any proper humidity or temperature control, and the so-called vinegar syndrome had already ravaged the collection. These films were produced under the Ordre Baru (New Order) of the military dictator Suharto, who ruled Indonesia from 1967 until 1998. During this period, film and television production were state controlled in order to silence oppositional voices. The rotting reels left at the PFN site reflected Indonesia's history in two ways: as a stockpile of propaganda material and as evidence of the total lack of courage to deal with such a toxic legacy. Edwin's discovery led to the formation of a collective that organised a series of workshops, screenings, and exhibitions based on the stockpile of prints and negatives (see figure 6.2). Not only did this collective gain access to the site but they also revived the film-printing facility with the technical support of Australians Richard Tuohy, Dianna Barrie, and Carl Looper. In an article for *Desistfilm*, an online platform dedicated to independent and experimental cinema, Lauren Bliss comments on one of the projection events:

They do not embed a 'moral message' in the propaganda films as they rescreen them, or offer a prior interpretation through which the film is to be understood in those that they rework and artistically manipulate – rather, it is the simple 'act of projection' through which the viewer is invited to engage and participate in order to come to terms with the materiality of perception. (Bliss, 2016)

Figure 6.2 Lab Laba Laba (ID 2015); photograph by Edwin.

This makes clear that the members of Lab Laba Laba did not engage with the films in a didactic way but rather wanted to share these now peculiar artefacts with an audience that had virtually no access to their own cultural and political past. However distressing Indonesia's era of murderous dictatorship may be, ignoring it will not make the pain go away. Lab Laba Laba's subsequent activities demonstrate that the artists involved were acutely aware of this situation, as evidenced by Luthfan Nur Rochman's installation *Excavating Memoirs* (2015), in which the artist embeds the continuous projection of one of the archive's films in an installation centred around an excavated skeleton. Lab Laba Laba also established contact with the European network of artist-run film labs and invited Grenoble-based filmmaker Etienne Caire for a residency in Jakarta. The residency resulted in the intense projection performance *Riuh Saudara / Vociferous Family* (2018), in which Caire and his fellow performers Joyce Lainé and Loïc Verdillon (stage names Riojim, Lucrecia, and Cool Verdict) confront the spectator with a barrage of images, both archival and new. The performance overwrites the image of Indonesia as an exotic paradise and instead shows a chaotic urban reality interlaced with photochemical manipulations and shattered fragments of South East Asian popular culture.

These examples demonstrate how the efforts of experimental film-makers to engage with archival activities are connected with broader social and political issues like the sustained dominance of Western culture and history and the marginalisation of communities. Efforts to reclaim photochemical film as an artistic medium are intertwined with the struggle to counteract the global dominance of a commodified media landscape in which the same stories keep on being repeated. Simultaneously, the continued use of photochemical film counteracts the concept of linear technological progress. Instead of an accelerated process in which tools and materials become obsolete in a gruelling race for efficiency, speed, superficial perfection, and individual success, the contemporary practice of handmade experimental filmmaking offers a slower, tactile, grounded, and community-based environment. Many artists who are part of this movement are well aware of the existential threat that constantly hovers over their medium and practice of choice. But in addition to the difficulties that this situation presents, there is also a bonus. Being attuned to break-down and the loss of control, these artists have become experts in making work about disaster, collapse, disappearance, and malfunction.

A good example of this approach is Tomonari Nishikawa's film *Sound of a Million Insects, Light of a Thousand Stars* (2014). The filmmaker provides the following statement on his website:

I buried a 100-foot (about 30 meters) 35mm negative film under fallen leaves alongside a country road, which was about 25 km away from the Fukushima Daiichi Nuclear Power Station, for about 6 hours, from the sunset of June 24, 2014, to the sunrise of the following day. The night was beautiful with a starry sky, and numerous summer insects were singing loud. The area was once an evacuation zone, but now people live there after the removal of the contaminated soil. This film was exposed to the possible remaining of the radioactive materials. (Nishikawa, 2021)

A shorter version of the same statement appears at the end of the two-minute film. This testimony provides the spectator with a framework that adds a layer onto the actual viewing experience itself while also complicating the poetic title of the film. The result of the process the artist describes is an abstract blue field that is increasingly disturbed by the exposure of the raw 35mm footage to hazardous environmental conditions. First, wriggly lines and dust particles appear while the blue field subtly changes in intensity and colour saturation, and then a second layer becomes visible, scratchier and darker than the first. Toward the end of the film, the impression of a monochrome blue field is destroyed by the sheer amount of abstract visual disturbance. The images are accompanied by a soft crackling sound that is caused by the same alterations of the photochemical emulsion. Corresponding to the changes in the image, the sound also increases in intensity, vanishing abruptly at the end of the buried roll. Without having further knowledge about the process, the location, and the nuclear accident at Fukushima, most spectators would be at a loss to interpret the work. But the artist's statement that is revealed at the end of the film changes this profoundly. It dawns on the spectator that film is a fragile material that will be impacted by radioactivity, just like the fogged photo that was taken from a helicopter fourteen hours after the explosion of the No. 4 reactor in the Chernobyl Nuclear Power Plant on 26 April 1986. The significance of something abstract and seemingly pointless like the fogging of photographic material is made comprehensible by Tess Takahashi in her article that analyses Nishikawa's film in the context of data visualisation:

Abstraction operates like a linguistic shifter, a representational box into which many things can be placed, and yet which is linked to something specific in the world. Contained scientific abstractions like the dot, the line, the number, the pointing finger, the geometric shape of the box, or the cinematic frame can be made to simultaneously indicate anything at all and to index a specific thing or idea. At the same time, in its ability to be filled, other things come rushing into it, such as the magnitude of emotion, disaster, loss – the enormity that easily overflows that box. (Takahashi, 2021: 74)

The abstract interferences in *Sound of a Million Insects, Light of a Thousand Stars* push in an unostentatious but decisive manner against the unspecified quality of the cinematic frame, making sense of the void left by an unimaginable disaster such as the meltdown of the Fukushima Daiichi reactor.

This movement from the unspecific to the epic also appears in Anja Dornieden and Juan David González Monroy's film *Wolkenschatten* (2014). Their film starts with a completely black frame accompanied by a voice-over (in German, with English subtitles) embedded in atmospheric synthesiser chords. The voice persuades the spectators to embark on a journey to a chimerical place. The first image that appears is a still picture of a pine forest, synecdochally standing for such a location. Like Takahashi's representational box, this image gradually embodies loss and pain. After the scene is set in such a foreboding way, the images are edited in more rapid succession, and the narrative coincides briefly with the visual representations. People enter a cave that leads to a bright clearing. Pain and loss are replaced by blissful ignorance. The gathered crowd embarks on a ritual centred around a machine – a machine that feeds the eyes. A strangeness creeps into the images, prompted by their material degradation as well as by superimpositions (see figure 6.3). The voice-over invites us to leave our bodies, minds, and memories behind, in order to 'disappear' into the images. Only the eyes remain as universal organs, prevailing in a powerful alliance with the machine. The machine, however, needs to be fed with our memories in a Faustian pact that turns into something horrific. The film ends with the head of a decapitated child telling a joke, leaving the spectators with a complex set of feelings during the final moments of the film. In an interview by Clint Enns published in *INCITE*, an artist-run publication dedicated to

Figure 6.3 *Wolkenschatten* – Anja Dornieden & Juan David González Monroy (DE 2014, 16mm film, colour, 17min); courtesy of the artists.

experimental film, video, and new media, Monroy provides the following comment:

Basically, cinema is a machine that talks to you, tells you a story. Given the dynamics of the cinema, the machine is programmed by the filmmakers to personally talk to each individual member of the audience. We started thinking about cinema this way by accident, but since this is what cinema in essence does, we thought we would focus on that aspect of it. Of course, the machine might be insane, it might be lying, it might be trying to convince you of different ways to view the world, or it might just be trying to entertain you by telling you a good story. (Enns, 2015)

Wolkenschatten does all of that at the same time with its bizarre and horrific story, surreal imagery, and tactile materiality. The seductive illusory power of the cinematic apparatus is taken into darker territory via the folding of a reflexive narrative about the medium into an imagined horrific experiment involving the eyes of the dead. The film seduces and repels the spectator, ingeniously invoking a phenomenological and an intellectual experience at the same time. The loss of memory and the disappearance of the image are presented as a blessing in disguise, making it possible to feel joy after a harrowing event. As with the reuse of propaganda films by the participating artists of Lab Laba Laba's archival project, there is no moral message forced onto the spectator. *Wolkenschatten* rather confounds, opening up possible new ways of seeing and experiencing cinema.

In 2002, the Dutch Filmmuseum curated a series of events around the colonial history shared by the Netherlands and Indonesia. I was given the opportunity to work on *A Journey to Tarakan* (2002), a personal documentary following my uncle's footsteps during his fatal involvement in the battle of Tarakan in 1942. In my documentary, I weave together a variety of archive materials with my own footage (shot on Super 8 film). The film could be described as a 'home movie' away from home, as much of the footage used in the film is shot by nonprofessionals, and my own Super 8 footage is predominantly shot with a handheld camera, spontaneously and without a script. Bringing together different sources and formats proved to be complicated and time-consuming and was only made possible thanks to the expertise of the film archivists I was working with. After getting acquainted with the challenges of restoring and preserving film, I started to wonder about the limits of preservation, and in 2010 I proposed to work on a project focused on a 'borderline' artefact from the archive. Instead of this being a traditional preservation effort, I was primarily interested in the dividing line between the visible and the invisible. In response, Simona Monizza and Mark-Paul Meyer, my partners at the archive, proposed that I could work with a recently found copy of *Haarlem* (1922), a commercial film made by Dutch film pioneer Willy Mullens. Originally, this film was intended as a form of 'city branding' to entice tourists to visit the attractive old city centre of this municipality in the Netherlands. The print in question was found in an archive in Italy, where the film must have ended up after being screened to an audience of potential sightseers. The nitrate material was in an advanced state of decomposition as a result of biodeterioration, shrinkage, and emulsion breakdown. Each form of deterioration had created particular effects. The bacteria that were growing on the film looked like mushroom clouds, the shrinkage had warped the entire film, and the emulsion breakdown had created a further deformation of the emulsion, in some cases resulting in tears and blisters. Working with a high-resolution digital scan of the film and an optical flow algorithm, I isolated, enlarged, and slowed down these deformations. The visual 'melt down' of the image inspired me to choose the title *Liquidator* (2010). I used the output of this process to recompose the entire film while maintaining its original duration. At the time when I was making and promoting the film, the Fukushima nuclear accident and the Wikileaks diplomatic cables leak dominated the news. Both events provided an interesting context for me to think about my project. Nuclear radiation is a force that distorts and alters living tissues in a drastic and unrepairable way. The Wikileaks website and community are a force that exposes hidden truths, revealing repression and corruption. Nitrate decay is usually cast as an accident, while the scale of this problem is so widespread that it can be called disastrous. However, the fractured images of a decaying roll of nitrate film actually have a truthful relationship with reality. The photographic image is as real as the traces that are left on the film by microorganisms and chemical decomposition. It was this 'documentary' aspect that revealed a hidden truth. Especially in the case of this print, these processes had acted as intruders, subverting the commercial content of Mullens's project. Instead of actively disrupting or destroying the images, a common practice in experimental filmmaking, I acted like a biographer of the material and the biological protagonists, presenting these unruly elements as a creative force in their own right.

The process described above – called 'biodeterioration' by film archivists – is turned into a methodology by Jennifer Reeves in her film *Landfill 16* (2011). Horrified by the bulk of outtakes left over after she finished her feature-length double projection *When It Was Blue* (2008), Reeves decided to recycle her footage, approaching her own footage as an archive which is first abandoned and subsequently recovered. The film material was temporarily buried, and the images were thus deliberately exposed to the transformative power of enzymes and fungi. After two months, the films were exhumed and rearranged through a further process of colouring, staining, and rephotographing. The final work confronts the spectator with a whirlwind of colour and dancing particles underscored by a soundtrack of industrial and mechanical noises that are mixed with field recordings. As a result of this process of layering, mixing, and alternating images and sounds, an array of different elements are intertwined into a unified experience. The textures and particles have an organic or cosmic quality reminiscent of a snow or dust storm, the cracked surface of dried-out soil, lichen growing on boulders, or stars and nebulae as seen through a telescope. The images also suggest a connection with abstract expressionist paintings by virtue of the bright colours and the seemingly gestural distribution of shapes. From this complex field of signals, the decipherable movements of a deer, an eagle, and a spider come into view, remaining after the onslaught of othering forces. Gregory Zinman offers a relevant comment:

Intentionally or not, Reeve's film offers a rebuke to any materialist romanticization of analog film. After all, film stock is made of plastic, and its emulsion is made with gelatin, which is derived from animal by-products. Therefore, when the film is buried in a landfill, it is not being destroyed or degraded so much as it is communing with the same elements that led to its manufacture. Its placement in and removal from the garbage is thus both a journey and a return. (Zinman, 2020: 118)

Reeves uses biodeterioration not as a destructive but as a creative intervention that is absorbed in the work. The material reality of the film competes with the photographed reality that was the focus of the footage before it was reworked. But instead of one prevailing over the other, the two realities fold into a site of ambiguity in which the spectator loses their sense of dimension and orientation. The borders between the real and the imagined, the spoiled and the pristine, and the physical and the mental are blurred. *Landfill 16* shares this disruptive approach with the other films discussed within this chapter. Instead of trying to preserve and fix memory, time, and truth, these films resonate with Donna Haraway's insight that in order to deal with the multiple crises of the present, 'staying with the trouble' might be the best strategy (Haraway, 2016: 1). In this particular case, that's the trouble of a material that is in constant flux, a medium that is in jeopardy of dying out, and a geopolitically, economically, and environmentally unstable world. The unexpected vibrancy that can be seen in the field of contemporary experimental film is hopeful, pointing toward an imperfect but still resilient and fruitful present.

7

Information Threshold

I have been intrigued for a long time by the differences in image structure between the digital and the photochemical image. When people questioned my continued use of photochemical film, I had no better argument than saying 'I like film grain'. The most obvious point that can be made about 'digital' and 'analog' media is that pixels are organised in a two-dimensional grid-like structure and film grain is randomly distributed in multiple overlapping layers. This leads to the use of words such as 'synthetic' and 'organic' to describe the differences between the respective media. However, such simple juxtapositions are not satisfactory to my mind. A possible way to explore the significance of the film grain further is to think in terms of 'faktura', a Russian word that was originally used to describe the quality of brushstrokes in icon painting. The meaning of the term was extended by avant-garde artists and critics in the 1910s to describe the quality of materials and processes other than painting. The Latvian painter and art critic Voldemārs Matvejs, an influential figure at the time, stretches the original meaning of 'faktura' by quoting an old Russian proverb: 'The saying is true that when people fall silent, stones will begin to speak' (Gough, 1999: 33). He subsequently argues that meaning is not created by the artist alone, but is brought out through an active process of transformation. The artist is seen as a medium who translates the inherit qualities of materials into form. This implies that materials contain (indexical) stories that potentially can be listened to. By arranging for heterogeneous materials to meet, a further dialectical process is set in motion. Keeping this idea in mind helps me to explore film grain as a formative element and extend my answer beyond a simple 'like'.

The graininess of photochemical emulsion provides an empty canvas with a very specific quality. Filmmakers such as Jennifer Reeves and

Tomonari Nishikawa welcome this specificity within their work, integrating the dynamic texture of tiny particles that seem to dance on the screen in their material explorations. However, the appearance of film grain is not always seen as an advantage. On the contrary, film grain is often described as unwanted noise to be avoided or removed. Digital technology is sometimes seen as the ultimate solution, especially after the development of ultra-high resolution and sophisticated software for film grain removal. Recently, this point of view has been questioned by a growing group of film directors who have argued in favour of film grain as an aesthetically desirable quality. As a result of this discussion, film grain removal has been followed by film grain synthesis within the digital workflow. In a technical article about this development, the authors first described how the physical process of developing emulsion results in 'tiny gaps' between the metallic silver particles that are embedded within gelatine. Furthermore, they postulate that

film grain appearance is therefore inevitable because of the physical nature of the process embedded in the film design itself. However, historically, it was considered as noise, and as such, technological advances have gone in the direction of its elimination. With the arrival and evolution of digital camera sensors, film grain no longer exists. Moreover, digital imaging offered many more advantages in terms of robustness, reproducibility, and above all visual quality. (Ameur et al., 2022: 1)

Within the context of this chapter, I explore both the historic perception of noise and the visual quality of the image. As noted in the quote above, photographers and filmmakers regularly find 'digital content too clean and sharp'. This observation implies that a more chaotic and fuzzy image quality may be advantageous under certain circumstances. The discussion concerning the right approach to represent reality has a very long history. Famously, Leonardo da Vinci developed a theoretical and practical approach to this problem, known as *sfumato*, capturing the usefulness of haze or smoke. Instead of using distinct lines and separations, the artist obscured the edges of forms and the transitions of colours and shadows. Art historian Janis Bell proposes that '*sfumato* is both a technique and a perception' (Bell, 2008: 162) This proposition is important as it relates not only to an external, objective reality but also to the subjectivity of perception. Bell underlines the importance of Leonardo's innovation:

Leonardo expanded the idea of perspective to the entire range of visual possibilities. He recognized no disjuncture between accurate vision and erroneous vision. Visual perception was a dynamic process, one in which there was continual interplay from the whole to the parts and vice versa. (Ibid., 164)

In his influential book about the psychology of perception, art historian Ernst Gombrich confirms this point of view while also highlighting the importance of the limitations of the artistic medium and the artist's ability to use such shortcomings imaginatively:

The amount of information reaching us from the visible world is incalculably large, and the artist's medium is inevitably restricted and granular. Even the most meticulous realist can accommodate only a limited number of marks on his panel, and though he may try to smooth out the transition between his dabs of paint beyond the threshold of visibility, in the end he will always have to rely on suggestion when it comes to representing the infinitely small. (Gombrich, 1995: 182–184)

Both art historians call attention to the interactive nature of spectatorship. It is not only the artist who uses their imagination in the process of making – the spectator in turn is enticed to complete the dynamic process of perception, representation, and interpretation in their own way. Rather than presenting the spectator with a final 'perfect' representation of reality, art mediates between objectivity and subjectivity. This helps to explain the ongoing appreciation of unfocused and grainy images by artists and audiences.

Besides the limitations of the artistic medium, as mentioned by Gombrich, the human brain itself is also not free of disturbances. Neuroscientists are increasingly interested in the brain's resting state and the remaining signals that are still present without external stimuli. Previously, it was assumed that the so-called global signal could simply be ignored. Therefore, the removal of the global signal is still a common practice in brain research. However, the discovery of triggers within this global signal has led to a lively debate about this approach (see further Murphy & Fox, 2017). The experience of a new thought that pops up from the muddled and grainy state of a resting brain is certainly not unfamiliar. The renowned experimental psychologist Richard Gregory has done research into a related phenomenon, exploring the boundary of the visible and the internal 'noise' that is generated by the visual cortex. His findings have led him to conclude that there is no absolute visual threshold:

The idea that discrimination is limited by noise in the nervous system has far-reaching consequences. It suggests that the old idea of a *threshold* intensity, above which stimuli need to be if they are to have any effect on the nervous system, is wrong. We now think of any stimulus as having an effect on the nervous system, but only being accepted as a signal of an event when the neural activity is unlikely to be merely a chance increase in the noise level. (Gregory, 1997: 95)

The ultimate boundary of vision is therefore not absolute but context dependent, which makes it an interesting area for artists to explore and exploit. Signals can be hidden within noise, protruding out of the background only when the circumstances are favourable. This is not something that happens only internally in the brain, or within the grainy surface of photochemical film on a microscopic scale; something similar can be observed on a cosmological scale:

Arno Penzias and Robert Wilson were working at the Bell Telephone Laboratories in New Jersey attempting to account for electrical noise that was limiting the sensitivity of commercial short-wave radio communications. They used a horn antenna that could be pointed anywhere in the sky [...]. After eliminating all other possibilities they concluded that their equipment was receiving faint radio signals from beyond the Galaxy that seemed to be the same in every direction they looked at. (Wynn-Williams, 2016: 87)

The supposed electrical noise or radio signals mentioned here are presently known as the Cosmic Microwave Background, a type of ancient radiation that has helped scientists to estimate the age and composition of the universe. Infinitesimally small fluctuations in this noise signal carry meaningful information that is of high value for scientists who work in the field of astronomy and astrophysics.

Perhaps the concept of noise is best known in the arts within the realm of music. In the twentieth century, the exploration of noise as sound and noise as music has gained a prominent place in history due to experiments by artists and composers such as Luigi Russolo, Edgar Varèse, Eric Satie, Pierre Schaeffer, and John Cage. In popular music too, noise has been explored extensively, both by commercially successful rock bands such as Nirvana and in much more confrontational ways, as exemplified by the work of the Japanese noise artist Masami Akita, a.k.a. Merzbow. In a meticulous investigation of the work of this radical practitioner, Paul Hegarty first reminds us that 'generally speaking, noise is taken to be a problem: unwanted sound, unorganised sound, excessively loud sound' (Hegarty, 2009: 193). However, noise has been brought into the realm of music in a number of ways, notably by John Cage's experiments with silence which resulted in the various noisy elements of our environment getting heard. But even before this contemporary rethinking of sound, music, and silence, 'noise has been seen as something more natural than music' (ibid.). Any sort of movement or turbulence will produce noise in the very media that we are embedded in and of which we are constituted. The atmosphere and surface water are always in motion, and likewise our blood circulates continuously as long as we are alive; even the liquid core of the earth itself is in constant motion. All of these movements create noise, a type of noise that is certainly not unwanted. 'So in the end, noise tells us we are alive – and to a large extent the functioning of these noises is beyond our conscious control' (ibid., 194).

While the above argument can also function within the visual realm, the presence of noise as a formative element is much less obvious within the visual arts. There is no visual equivalent to 'noise music', at least not under such a definitive banner. Further analysing the layers of meaning connected to the word 'noise' can help us explore the pervasiveness of noise within the visual field. As argued by Vinícius Portella Castro, noise manifests in three distinct phases – firstly, as 'a technical impediment in the transmission of information' (Castro, 2022: 3). An example of this would be the unwanted grainy appearance of photochemical film that this chapter started with. But that same example immediately brings us to the next phase, namely, 'the cumulative series of technical and natural contingencies that constituted that event' (ibid., 5). As we have seen, film grain is often perceived as an unwanted element, but the appearance of film grain is 'inevitable because of the physical nature of the process embedded in the film design itself' (Ameur et al, 2022: 1). In other words, the technical makeup of photochemical emulsion and the natural contingency therein will inevitably lead to a certain amount of graininess within the image. This explains why analog film is often described as being 'organic', as opposed to the presumed 'synthetic' nature of the digital image. Beyond the 'technical impediment' and the 'natural contingencies', Castro arrives at a third phase of understanding noise: 'the channel that modulates energy to carry the signal also carries noisy thermal entropy along the way' (Castro, 2022: 6). A clear example of this proposition is the Cosmic Microwave Background, initially understood as noise but actually carrying a truckload of information when looked at more carefully. Castro uses this third entropic phase to suggest an ingrained creative and generative potential:

Invention always comes out of the noisy margin of indeterminacy, forms always come from the background that harbors their generative dynamisms. Information is never decided beforehand, it is always a concrete and contingent transformation between systems. No cast of the die can abolish noise. (Ibid., 7)

In her groundbreaking analysis of the information age, Katherine Hayles argues along a similar line of thought:

Identifying information with *both* pattern and randomness proved to be a powerful paradox, leading to the realization that in some instances, an infusion of noise into a system can cause it to reorganize at a higher level of complexity. Within such a system, pattern and randomness are bound together in a complex dialectic that makes them not so much opposites as complements or supplements to one another. Each helps to define the other; each contributes to the flow of information through the system. (Hayles, 1999: 25)

Subsequently, in order to explore this proposition further, she asks herself an intriguing question: 'When and how does this noise coalesce into pattern?' (ibid., 27). This leads us back to experimental filmmakers and their relentless artistic explorations of both the limits of medium and the limits of perception.

In the previously discussed expanded cinema performance *Alchemie* by Jürgen Reble and Thomas Köner, a noisy field of film grain coalesces into a sequence of images only to break down into noise again. Reble uses alchemy and the alchemists as a reference in his explorations of chemical alteration of the moving image. The American experimental filmmaker Phil Solomon has been working within this field as well. While Reble is focused on a form of visual music bordering on the abstract, Solomon integrates his chemical experiments within a lyrical, narrative structure. His film *Remains to Be Seen* (1989),made in remembrance of his mother, uses the chemical treatment of the images as a metaphor for fading memories and the failing of the body. Solomon does not use head or tail titles because he wants 'visions to come on and recede, oceanic, vaporous, organic' (Rossin, 2007). The film starts with shimmering fields of white particles on a dark blue and black background. Within this background foliage, a mountain range, a room, and a swimmer can be perceived. The white particles intensify, briefly erasing the entire image. Next, a patient on a stretcher and the caring hands of a clinician can be clearly seen through the swirling specks of white (see figure 7.1). A cross-modal or even synesthetic experience is created by the mingling of the noisy sounds of wind, water, an indistinct voice, and an artificial lung. The opening sequence continues with a back and forth between the two themes: landscape and hospital. Some of the landscape imagery moves toward abstraction, briefly coalescing back into somewhat more distinct images of foliage and water. Angelic voices are introduced in the second sequence, which is composed of travelling shots again intercut with the hospital footage. The sound of window wipers seems to connect with the sound of the artificial lung, providing an

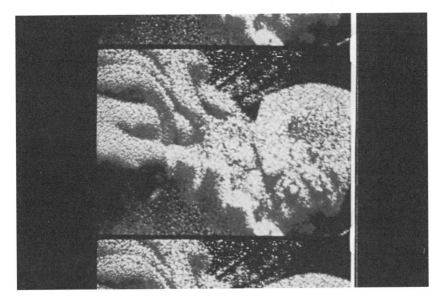

Figure 7.1 *Remains to Be Seen* – Phil Solomon (CA 1989, 16mm film, colour, 17min); courtesy of the Phil Solomon Project.

existential undertone to the commonplace images of a road and a passing landscape. The white particles now recall the experience of looking
through a rain-speckled window. Again, images of the landscape and the
hospital are woven together, degraded toward the brink of abstraction.
A calmly walking figure provides a counterpoint to the seething brew of
emulsion. The introduction of a beeping sound punctures the hypnotic
stream of images, bringing us back to the tense reality of an intensive care
unit. After this short intermission, a heavily reverberating piano accompa-
nies almost dreamlike home-movie footage ending in black. A crackling
sound now changes the spectators' perception of the landscape impressions from wet, cold, and rainy to dry, hot, and sunny. Light filters through
rustling leaves and reflects off the surface of a building. Hovering voices lift
these images into an unearthly experience. Figures pass casually through
the frame, their upper bodies radiating with light. The hospital footage
reaches a climax with an image of a beating heart, accompanied by the
uneasy beeping of a medical device. Shadowy figures are washed from the
screen. Upon their return, the noisy sounds now have a much more sinister character. The beeping sound returns for a third and a fourth time, now
highly irregular. In the final sequence, birds fly across the screen and two
figures appear, one standing, the other one walking away. Throughout the
film, Solomon uses noise in sound and image as a signifier of both pattern
and randomness. Noisy images appear as relating to rain, sunlight, and the
patterns that are sometimes produced by the visual system without being
triggered by an external stimulus. Noisy sounds appear as related to wind,
water, urban noise, and hospital noise. Alternatively, noisy images and
sounds relate to the breakdown of the senses of a patient on the brink of
life and death. Finally, the noise in *Remains to Be Seen* also calls forth the
subliminal sensation of consciousness slipping away and memories fading. In an article about the filmmaker in the Canadian magazine *Cinema
Scope*, Michael Sicinski writes:

A figure in a Solomon film never entirely vanishes into the primordial soup, but
is instead subjected to an oscillation between presence and absence, wherein
his or her physical boundaries and the surrounding space become intertwined –
individual identity becoming an unstable isotope. (Sincinski, 2007: 32)

Such an 'oscillation between presence and absence' is not only acted out
on screen but is also relayed to the spectator. The shimmering images that

appear out of and vanish back into what Sicinski calls 'primordial soup' challenge the visual perception of the spectator by approaching and crossing over the threshold of the intelligible. This 'noisy margin of indeterminacy', to go back to Castro, functions as a point of breakdown and a point of revelation. In *Remains to Be Seen*, the transition between life and death is simultaneously unsettling and comforting, leading to a period of mourning for those who remain and promising a unification with nature for the deceased. The spectator is given the possibility to empathise with both.

The visual noise produced by Solomon is achieved by a process of chemical degradation. The filmmaker has described his own process like this: 'I'm something of an archaeologist in reverse: I try to discover truths in these artefacts by throwing the dirt back on them. I bury things rather than excavate them' (MacDonald, 2006: 219–220). Layers of material and optical distortion are added to the original footage in order to question their meaningfulness. However, noisy images can also be achieved through a different route. Takashi Makino, a Japanese experimental filmmaker, has dedicated much of his work to the investigation of patterns and randomness. In one of his early works, the fifty-one minute-long film *The World* (2009), the subject is explored through the lens of a 16mm camera. The film consists primarily of images of foliage, water, and clouds. At the end of the film, some urban footage is also included. By zooming in on details, including out-of-focus shots, pointing the camera in the direction of the sun, panning or moving in diagonals, upside-down imagery, negative images, and multiple exposures, Makino presents the ordinary as something close to abstraction. Textures are formed and unravel. Phenomenological sensations such as fluidity, gaseousness, and solidity are aroused. Light breaks through darkness, and complex patterns of light and dark seem to be engaged in a playful game. Cracks open and close, forms pulsate, streaks shoot across the screen. Eventually, the light folds back into shades and cavities, covered gently with layers of darkness. In Makino's sixty-minute-long film *Memento Stella* (2018), the raw footage has been recorded with a modified digital camera. Again, images of snow, water, foliage, and buildings are used as source material. Through the superimposition of an abundance of layers (up to 200), their representational quality is practically removed (see figure 7.2). The spectator is confronted with an abstract field of dots, lines, and colours in flux. Instead of cutting from shot to shot, the images change gradually, and the film can

Figure 7.2 *Memento Stella* – Takashi Makino (JP 2018, 4K video, colour, 60 min); courtesy of the artist.

be experienced as one sixty-minute take. The speed of change varies, and some changes are almost imperceptible and register only after a certain amount of time has passed. Other changes are more sudden, like a cloud passing in front of the sun. The film starts with tiny light spots that seem to emanate from the centre of the screen, creating the illusion of movement and space. The balance between light and dark slowly shifts, until the light blinds the spectator. Rhythm and movement suddenly become unstable, and light quickly ebbs away. Within this sequence, hints of clouds and water appear but the source of the images is never fully revealed. Later in the film, forms that could have a human origin seem to wander over the screen, thick foliage seems to travel overhead, and angular patterns call forth man-made structures. On his website, Makino clarifies his goal:

> Rather than making films with my own imposed structure, my method is to abandon structure altogether or, in other words, layer images that once embodied meaning on top of one another until they become unintelligible. I aim for the resulting composite 'image' to be like a nameless animate being with a limitless capacity for meanings, so that my films become triggers for an audience to venture into their own imagination. (Makino, n.d.)

Reinier van Houdt's soundtrack to *Memento Stella* enhances this 'capacity for meanings' through layers of noise, sustained notes, and dispersed piano sounds. The Dutch pianist and composer writes about his approach: 'Music seems more like a natural phenomenon or a ghostlike apparition, brought about by experiments or certain states of mind. Heavily distorted or barely audible – a hiss, almost; an essential unreliability, that nevertheless determines its vitality' (van Houdt, n.d.). Noise is certainly not unwanted or unorganised in either Makino's or van Houdt's work; rather, noise functions here as a source from which meaning can spring. This analogy seems particularly apt as Makino repeatedly uses a movement that originates in the centre of the screen and subsequently moves toward the edges. This creates the illusion of something bubbling up or coming toward the viewer. Simultaneously, such a centralised point makes it easier for the spectator to focus their attention and let the abstraction wash over them like a river. Instead of a narrative or an objective meaning, the perceptive spectator is provided with an open invitation to explore the meaning-making capacity of their senses, visual apparatus, brain, body, and mind.

With my film *Wilderness Series* (2016), I attempted to achieve a similar result while starting from the other end. Instead of altering representational footage to such an extent that it becomes abstract, I started with nonrepresentational camera-less footage. The images were made on expired 35mm film aided by organic materials and processes and therefore have a very direct and real relationship to the world. I chose to work on expired film in order to minimise the environmental footprint of my actions. My intention was to 'grow' an image instead of degrading existing material. Image degradation is a recurring element in experimental film, either simply driven by time, as in the previously discussed found-footage films (Delpeut, Morrison), or imposed by the filmmaker through burying the film (Reeves), treating it with corrosive chemistry (Reble, Solomon), scratching it, or via other methods. My aim was to explore the possible *generation* of images by means of chemical treatment. Informed by the desire to reduce waste and energy, I was aiming to keep things as local as possible. By all appearances, my urban environment was not the most obvious location for finding organic materials. However, cities are full of microbial, fungal, and plant live. Even certain animals thrive within cities, and the number of animals is actually increasing due to human encroachment on their natural habitat. My first experiment was simple: I picked up the fallen leaves of the plane trees that have been planted along many London roads and wrapped these in a roll of unexposed film. After a few days, I carefully unwrapped the leaves and processed the film in a coffee-based developer (see Williams, 1995). The leaves had created a pattern on the film's emulsion: sometimes clearly recognisable imprints, sometimes seemingly autonomous or random ones. For my second experiment, I gathered a bottle full of sludge from Deptford Creek, the lower part of the River Ravensbourne, one of the few tributaries of the Thames that has not been completely embanked. The mudbanks next to the creek are within reach of the tides but can be explored on foot during low tide. The mud is teeming with microbes and invertebrates, which made it a good source for my experiment. I covered 35mm film with this sludge, again leaving the treated film exposed for a number of days. When I cleaned and developed the film, labyrinthian patches of brown and red appeared, punctured by white dots and bigger slashes of white. For my third experiment, I used mushrooms, cutting the stems and arranging the caps with gills down on a moist strip of film. This resulted in green, yellow, and black clouds and cuts in the emulsion. Here and there, the emulsion had come loose, folding back in jagged shapes. After this, I infused a strip of film with salt water. After I dried and developed it, a complex pattern emerged on the filmstrip. The caustic properties of salt had formed crystalline shapes in the emulsion. The overall colour of this strip was green, but some yellow and red areas had formed as well. The final step was to use fresh green leaves. This idea was inspired by a recipe for a spearmint-based developer posted on a listserv by Portuguese filmmaker Ricardo Leite. Leite has done further research into biodegradable developers and has recently published his results in an online article (Leite, 2022). Inspired by his recipe, I concluded that it would be worthwhile to try to use the intact leaves instead of grinding the plant material. I soaked the fresh spearmint leaves in a solution of soda and vitamin C, using a basic caffenol recipe as my starting point. I covered a filmstrip with the steeped leaves, exposing the material for about twenty-four hours in a dark space. After the plants were removed, detailed patterns were visible on the film, showing the intricate structure of the leaves surrounded by crystallised chemistry. My laboratory approach was a process of discovery – I was deliberately renouncing control. The resulting patterns, textures, and colours had more in common with abstract expressionist paintings than images that are the result of lens-based photography (see figure 7.3). After I scanned the filmstrips on a high-resolution scanner, it became possible to search for patterns,

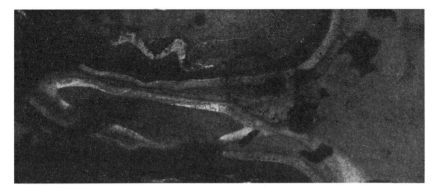

Figure 7.3 *Wilderness Series* – Karel Doing (UK 2016, 2K video, colour, 13min).

movements, and forms through a further process of framing, layering, and animating. I collaborated with the electroacoustic music composer Andrea Szigetvári during this post-production phase. In her work, she focuses on synchresis, the mental fusion between sound and image. To achieve this fusion for this particular project, she downloaded a library of free sounds from Yellowstone National Park (National Park Service, 2020). The sounds of geysers, vents, springs, and wildfires were cut up in small fragments and rearranged in parallel with the images. This rearrangement of both sound and image now guided the spectator through an extremely noisy field of images and sounds. Through the enhancement of patterns, the framing of recurring forms, the animation of movement, the creation of depth through layering, and the application of synchresis, the seemingly random specks, blots, smudges, and slashes that were visible on the original filmstrips now did convey a sense of signification. The hidden information in the noisy signal started to 'speak'.

In context of the desirability or undesirability of film grain, the films discussed above demonstrate how a grainy blank canvas can be a perfect starting point for those filmmakers who seek to express thoughts and feelings that are connected to the entropic forces that surround and pervade us. The film grain itself is a physical example of randomness and can simultaneously be conceived as an empty page receptive to all forms of information. Effectively, what I am suggesting here is a connection between the second law of thermodynamics and information theory. Here, another paradox appears. Information is primarily seen as the opposite of entropy.

More information equals more order. However, noise is potentially excessively rich in information as it is yet undefined (see further Malaspina, 2018) This paradox touches on the mystery of life itself: How can complex creatures such as ourselves emerge from chaos? This fundamental question can be approached in many different ways, either by looking inward at the workings of the brain or by looking outward and searching for the beginning of the universe. In both cases, noise is present, sometimes as a factor that hinders our understanding but also as an endless source of new information. In the arts, noise plays an equally important role in ever-changing and surprising ways. The experimental filmmaker's love for film grain is certainly not a nostalgic longing to revive a lost paradise but is rather driven by a fascination with the coexistence of order and chaos in our lives. Solomon's exploration of the threshold between life and death, Makino's exploration of the threshold between representation and abstraction, and my own exploration of the meaning-making capacity of natural processes demonstrate how awareness is not something that is fully formed in a particular instant. Out of a noisy field, an image appears, first on the very edge of perception and then, grain by grain, frame by frame, meaning is formed.

8

Roundtable

In 2012, I met Paolo Davanzo and Lisa Marr, who were in Rotterdam to work on a community project, a collectively made city symphony by and for a young generation of creatives. Their project was modelled on a previous iteration made in their home town, Los Angeles. They asked me to show my film *Images of a Moving City* (2001), a poetic and associative string of portraits and cityscapes shot in Rotterdam. Before the screening, I spoke about my sources of inspiration and the process of making this film. After the screening, I took questions from the group. There was an immediate connection between us, and I proposed to follow the entire project with a video camera, which would result in a 'making-of' to be broadcast on local television. During one of the initial gatherings, they screened the first iteration of what was to become a series of films, *The Sound We See: A Los Angeles City Symphony* (2010). One of the things that struck me was the bold reference to Dziga Vertov's *Man with a Movie Camera* (1929) in the opening titles (see figure 8.1). As I was about to leave the city after seventeen years and move to London, my life was in flux. The positive energy radiating from my new friends was extremely welcome, and I was impressed by their ability to build a coherent creative team within a few weeks' time. Instead of acting like directors or producers, Davanzo and Marr saw themselves as facilitators, and the workshop participants were all invited to contribute to the project on an equal basis. Such an approach is unusual in the highly hierarchically organised film industry and is not that common in the art world either. However, experimental filmmakers do work collaboratively, either as a performance group, as a collectively run film lab, or with musicians and sound artists. More radically, co-creation is embraced by some of these groups and collectives, and the traditional role of the director is renounced.

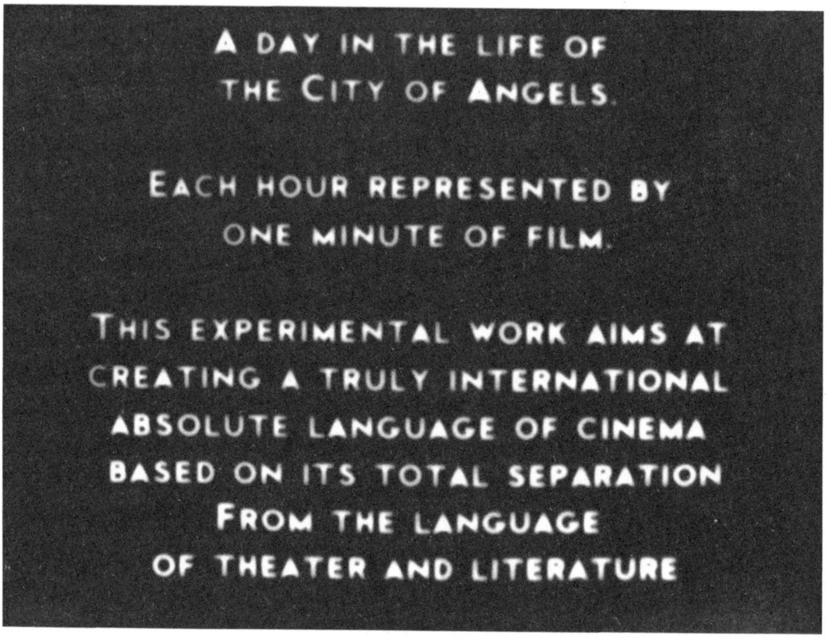

**A DAY IN THE LIFE OF
THE CITY OF ANGELS.**

**EACH HOUR REPRESENTED BY
ONE MINUTE OF FILM.**

**THIS EXPERIMENTAL WORK AIMS AT
CREATING A TRULY INTERNATIONAL
ABSOLUTE LANGUAGE OF CINEMA
BASED ON ITS TOTAL SEPARATION
FROM THE LANGUAGE
OF THEATER AND LITERATURE**

Figure 8.1 *The Sound We See: A Los Angeles City Symphony* – Echo Park Film Center (US 2010, 16mm film, bw, 27min); courtesy of the artists.

The following inquiry takes Vertov's masterpiece *Man with a Movie Camera* as a departure point and subsequently explores how co-creation can be used as an expressive element in experimental cinema. The question that is posed here is how Vertov's film can be used as a source of inspiration, both in terms of structure and methodology. To be able to answer this question, it is important for us to look at the original first. *Man with a Movie Camera* was made in an extraordinary, volatile time, a moment in history that still elicits a vision of hope and profound social change. A succinct and compelling statement concerning Vertov's visionary legacy can be found in the article 'Vertov after Manovich' by Seth Feldman:

Vertov is, after all, a citizen not just of the revolution but of the film of the revolution. From the beginning, his manifestoes, including the filmed manifesto of *Man with a Movie Camera,* posit cinema as a means of participation and that participation as a means of contributing to the revolution's new understanding of the world. (Feldman, 2007: 46)

The participation Feldman points at is not only realised by the appearance of the cameraman and the editor in the film, or by the great variety of people who appear in the film as themselves. It is also perceived by the spectators of the film, who are invited to participate in the production of meaning while watching the film. The signification of the film can be rephrased in almost endless variations, as the spectators are offered a semantic text in need of completion. This glorious 'incompleteness' renders the film contemporary, compatible with a mediated (postmodern) reality in which everything constantly changes form and meaning. But the film was certainly not intended for a select audience and their intellectual satisfaction – its purpose was to serve as a tool that would help to achieve the revolutionaries' dream of shared prosperity. From Vertov's manifestos, it becomes apparent that he envisioned an army of filmmakers who would adopt his method and numerous films would be made, advocating the communal message around the globe (Vertov & Michelson, 2001). Despite Vertov's productivity, manifested in numerous films and texts, he was not able to fulfil this goal:

His supporters, most of whom resided in the Soviet avant-garde outside of cinema, could be vocal, but the cineaste practitioners, the kinok armies, implied in his manifestos were largely imaginary. His manifestos and other proclamations picked hopeless fights with the rapidly ascending filmmakers and decision makers of the Soviet cinema establishment. Nor did his writing provide much in the way of concrete instructions for would-be followers (Feldman, 2007: 40).

Indeed, this army of documentary filmmakers did not materialise, in the Soviet Union or elsewhere. But the film has been highly influential in other ways. Apart from being seen as the progenitor of the 'city symphony' genre, *Man with a Movie Camera* is described as an important forebear of digital and interactive forms of storytelling by Lev Manovich in his book *The Language of New Media*, which is entirely structured around Vertov's film (Manovich 2001). Manovich phrases what Feldman calls 'participation' as a process of discovery and seduction: 'Vertov's goal is to seduce us into his way of seeing and thinking, to make us share his excitement, as he discovers a new language for film. This gradual process of discovery is the film's main narrative, and it is told through a catalog of discoveries' (ibid., 243). The insight that *Man with a Movie Camera* can be seen as driven by a catalogue or a database is key to Manovich's thinking. According to him, the database leads to nothing less than a new way to understand the world:

> Indeed, if after the death of God (Nietzsche), the end of grand Narratives of Enlightenment (Lyotard), and the arrival of the web (Tim Berners-Lee), the world appears to us as an endless and unstructured collection of images, texts, and other data records, it is only appropriate that we will be moved to model it as a database. But it is also appropriate that we would want to develop a poetics, aesthetics, and ethics of this database. (Ibid., 219)

But the main attraction of *Man with a Movie Camera* might not be its participative process or its database structure. What unfolds before our eyes is a vision of society – a society in which everybody has a role. A world full of joy, beauty, poetry, and dance. Not only the people who appear in the film seem to participate in a grand choreography, but the animals, vehicles, machines, and even buildings and objects are also part of a cinematic ballet. As such, the film draws us into a poetic understanding of the real. The film *prefigures* a utopian society as imagined by Vertov and his team. Herein lies its most powerful political statement, a statement that provides a starting point for Manovich's desired new poetics, aesthetics, and ethics. The concept of the prefigurative as a deliberate political strategy is derived from a groundbreaking article by sociologist Carl Boggs. Boggs analyses 'the troublesome dilemmas encountered by Marxist movements and regimes' (Boggs, 1977: 359) between the procurement of power and the implementation of a decentralised, fair, and inclusive form of democratic governance. Trying to reach utopia by brute force will result in the destruction of the desired future before it is even fully contemplated, as exemplified by Soviet Russia. Instead, the future needs to be rehearsed before it can be successfully applied in full scale. In *Prefigurative Politics: Building Tomorrow Today* (Raekstad & Gradin, 2020) the authors provide a further discussion of prefigurative politics. One of the objectives of this book is to clarify the term so that it's not used randomly. By analysing a number of sources, including anarchists like Mikhail Bakunin and Emma Goldman and organisations ranging from the Black Panthers to the Occupy Movement, the authors produce a concise definition of prefigurative politics: 'the *deliberate* experimental implementation of *desired* future social relations and practices in the here-and-now' (ibid., 36).

A relevant film to consider is the Russian production *I Love You / Я Тебя Люблю* (2011), an experimental documentary shot by a group of amateur videographers in the southern Russian city Rostov-on-Don. The directors describe the film as 'a democratic film about ordinary people', a statement that emphasises their independence from state-sponsored productions. Co-directors Rastorguev and Kostomarov collected their footage by casting a small group of participants from 1,673 respondents and asking the chosen protagonists to document their own lives. The directors shaped the final film out of the large catalogue of moving images that they received, kneading their narrative from a 'database' of material (Chapman, 2011). Although the film does not follow a 'dusk till dawn' structure, the objectives of the filmmakers overlap with Vertov's aim to capture actuality in a participatory way, as confirmed by the filmmakers in an online interview by independent scholar Anna Nieman: 'The sieve, the actual hole in the sieve was the un-robbed, un-castrated life, be it smart, or not, pretty, or not, kind, or not, but it has to be unwashed, raw, unprocessed, in the way it happens, unmediated by a film crew' (Nieman, 2013). Besides the raw characters, the cinematography is also 'raw', with frequent occurrences of auto-focus and auto-exposure adjustments, plus the use of accidental footage and chaotic camera angles. Similar to what Feldman describes as the seduction of the audience, here the spectator is persuaded to step into a tough post-communist reality. The camera witnesses the three main characters, who live in bare tower-block apartments and are either unemployed or toiling in repetitive jobs. Conversations revolve around the absence of future prospects, alcohol consumption, and harsh jokes, but the honesty and intimacy of the footage simultaneously shows how vulnerable and fragile the protagonists are and how much they depend on each other and their partners.

In *I Love You* we are confronted with a small army of disenfranchised workers looking for love and comfort in the new reality of rogue capitalism, which has replaced the now deflated utopia of Soviet communism. The main weapon of the cinematic soldiers is a camera, a digital machine that can accurately 'shoot' visual information. The absence of the communal is palpable, and is embodied by the toiling, swearing, and drinking of the main characters. If we can talk about poetics here, the directors deserve credit for achieving a balance between their forfeiture of control during the shooting and the recoupment of it during the editing phase, rhyming the crude footage into a refined whole. The film's ethics are also precarious, teetering on the voyeuristic, with its display of intimate imagery of the protagonists' relationships. But the directors succeed in respecting their characters all the way through. The film embraces a YouTube aesthetic that will offend some cinephiles but can be seen as affectionate to the concurrent moving image apparatus, the digital kino-eye. The film therefore comes much closer to Manovich's desired maturation of the database as a narrative tool. However, the key decisions in the filmmaking process are still dependent on the directors, as substantiated by them in the same interview: 'We have given them an opportunity to begin talking and then took their syntagms and assembled a coherent text' (ibid.). The documentary *I Love You* focuses on strong emotional experiences which are represented in unpolished footage. The film had limited success in the international festival circuit; it was mainly produced with a domestic audience in mind: 'For months they've toured Russia and Ukraine, appearing in-person at multiple screenings, conducting discussion panels and engaging with the audience' (ibid.). This form of independent, self-organised distribution is significant and important in regard to the effectiveness of the film's prefigurative elements. Screening the film in the specific cultural context in which it was conceived will make the participatory elements much more effective. Gestures and subtle cultural codes will be understood almost effortlessly, encouraging the audience to analyse and discuss the film with their peers. By actively involving both the protagonists and the audience, the co-directors have succeeded in taking the film beyond mere representation. In his article 'They Don't Represent Us? Synecdochal Representation and the Politics of Occupy Movements', Matthijs van de Sande highlights what is at stake here: 'The most significant difference between representation as *acting for* and representation as *standing for* is that the former often implies an explicit mandate and a certain degree of *responsiveness* between the representative and the thing represented' (van de Sande 2020: 401). This can be understood within the context of contemporary democracy (or semi-democracy), which often lacks responsiveness, subsequently not only undermining the relationships between politicians and voters but also having a further impact on the social fabric of society as a whole. Prefigurative politics attempts to restore this fabric by weaving new patterns. Instead of the utopian present prefigured in *Man with a Movie Camera*, the aim in *I Love You* seems to be more modest: to survive with dignity. The importance and relevance of such struggle is highlighted in John Holloway's analysis of the subject: 'Often the struggle of dignity is non-subordinate rather than openly insubordinate, often it is seen as private rather than in any sense political or anti-capitalist. Yet the non-subordinate struggle for dignity is the material substratum of hope' (Holloway 2019: 158).

A second example of a film that uses co-creation as an artistic strategy is *The Sound We See: A Los Angeles City Symphony*. This project was initiated by the Echo Park Film Center (EPFC), a non-profit media arts organisation established in 2002 offering film screenings, film classes, and equipment rentals and repairs (see further Rosales 2013). The film shows contemporary urban life in Los Angeles as seen through the eyes and cameras of the thirty-seven participating teenagers. As a starting point, the instructors, the EPFC youth education team, created a twenty-four-hour matrix for the students and asked them to choose both a time slot and a location. The students were instructed in the use of 16mm Bolex cameras and watched *Man with a Movie Camera* and associated films like Walter Ruttmann's *Berlin die Sinfonie der Großstadt* (*Berlin, Symphony of a Metropolis* 1927) and Joris Ivens's *Regen* (*Rain* 1929). Each team shot a modest amount of footage at their chosen time and location and, after processing, edited this down to one minute. The 24 sections were joined, and a live soundtrack was created by a local music group. *The Sound We See* starts with a title sequence echoing the opening credits of *Man with a Movie Camera*, but before cutting into action, the caption 'This is our City' appears on screen. In the first shot, we see the co-creators running enthusiastically through an urban tunnel sparsely lit by fluorescent lights (see figure 8.2). This functions both as an introduction to the episodes that follow and to the army of young aspiring filmmakers themselves. In the rest of the film, although their different styles and preoccupations can be detected, they remain largely unseen. In the subsequent scenes, contrasting locations in Los Angeles are covered: from Chinatown to a cement factory and from Hollywood Boulevard in the early hours, when only street cleaners are treading across the Walk of Fame, to a small urban gardening project hidden somewhere in the vast urban sprawl. Even though images

Figure 8.2 *The Sound We See: A Los Angeles City Symphony* – Echo Park Film Center (US 2010, 16mm film, bw, 27min); courtesy of the artists.

of Los Angeles continuously appear in popular movies, here the city shows a different face altogether. For example, the cyclists, homeless people, and musicians in the film are all authentic and caught off-guard by the camera. What we see is not an idealised 'larger than life' super-city, but a refreshingly 'real' Los Angeles seen from the point of view of each of the co-creators. After the initial success of this project, two of the instructors, Paolo Davanzo and Lisa Marr, have been leading twenty community filmmaking projects in cities around the world. This ongoing venture is documented online and links to a dedicated channel showcasing the whole series (Echo Park Film Center, 2020). The first episode was used as an educational tool in the subsequent iterations of the project, each time inspiring a new group of participants to partake in the creation of their own film. These films are successively screened in the city of their conception, often accompanied by live music. Additionally, the films are screened at the point of origin, the EPFC in Los Angeles. Finally, the films are released online to encourage further exchange. *The Sound We See: A Los Angeles City Symphony* is poetic as a result of its focus on everyday life and DIY approach to filmmaking. Prescribed by the low-budget approach, the scenes are shot with available light, resulting in footage with an atmospheric character. Similarly, due to the scarcity of film stock, shots are carefully chosen and composed. A reverence for time and place is imbued in the material, poetically capturing the mindset of the young participants. The precariousness of life in a vast urban sprawl is juxtaposed with moments of beauty and belonging. During classes, the instructors extensively use body language (reminiscent of the 'jazz hands' used by the Occupy movements), hands-on instruction, and group discussion as educational tools. Their enthusiasm, love for low-budget filmmaking, and positive outlook on life in general are all significant as prefigurative tools employed in the process of making.

The Sound We See: A Los Angeles City Symphony is a 'glocal' film, aware of the tensions and contradictions of contemporary city life. The community aspect of the project is taken very seriously: in addition to filming the actual footage, participants did their own editing and also had a say in further post-production decisions. All of this holds together successfully, supported by the twenty-four-hour grid and the continuous guidance and support of the project leaders, who run their centre (and externally affiliated groups) as a big family. The limitation of the project is delineated by this approach as well – the film does not achieve the critical social and political depth that is offered by *I Love You*. Instead, *The Sound We See* is a celebration of youthfulness and collaboration, and as such is successful in prefiguring 'desired social relations and practices' in a meaningful and coherent way. The key element here is education, in the sense of providing participants with power *to* (instead of power *over*). This is relevant in the light of Raekstad and Gradin's analysis of power relations and prefigurative politics: 'Being able to seize the means of production naturally requires you to have certain internal powers of your own – like the capacity to communicate with others and to know how certain machines work' (Raekstad & Gradin 2020: 42). Several of the participants who were involved in *The Sound We See: A Los Angeles City Symphony* are now working at the centre as instructors, educating the next generation. Others have been able to secure further education in the arts or creative industries. The aim here is practical: supporting the creative development of marginalised communities. But this objective is not approached in a linear way, separating methods from outcome. Instead, a more multidimensional system is used: a dialogical approach that includes instructors, participants, and spectators.

The third case study to be discussed is not one film but a collection of films, all made within the framework of the Independent Imaging Retreat or, more succinctly, Film Farm. The retreat is an initiative set up by teacher/filmmaker Philip Hoffman and the late writer/filmmaker Marian McMahon in 1994. The yearly gathering takes place at a rural farm in Ontario, deliberately taking the participants away from their urban dwellings (see figure 8.3). Film equipment is set up in the barn, and darkrooms are located in the area formerly occupied by animal pens. During the first few years, screenings took place upstairs while the cows mooed underneath. A series of workshops facilitates exchanges between filmmakers who have a variety of experience and skills. Footage is shot and developed without a preconceived plan, and the rough environment and sober production methods are reflected in the resulting images. A key workshop is focused on eco-processing, using plants and flowers from the yard and adjacent fields as ingredients to mix film developer. This eco-sensitivity is

Figure 8.3 Film Farm participants (CA 2015); courtesy of Phil Hoffman.

extended in workshops about natural tinting and toning techniques and phytography (see chapter 11). The resulting catalogue of works produced at the farm reflects the conditions in which the films were made: the rural surroundings, the old barn, the basic equipment, and the assembled aficionados. The Film Farm provides an environment which works not only as a backdrop or subject but also as a particular kind of disposition that becomes part of each film. A more extensive account of the retreat can be found in ' "An Arrow, Not a Target" ' (MacKenzie, 2013).

The individual films are not intended to form one unifying whole but are regularly screened together in constantly shifting combinations. An extensive list of completed films, now exceeding 100 titles, can be found on Hoffman's website (Hoffman, 2019). Recurring motifs such as the landscape, the vegetation, the buildings, the type of film stock, the processing method, the improvisational approach to filmmaking, and the communal and co-creational nature of the retreat appear in a variety of combinations. These motifs form a patchwork of interlocking parts in a grand narrative, only present in a subtext, pointing back at the source. Going back to Vertov's analogy of cinematic soldiers who fight to bring a new (utopian) reality into the world, the Film Farm could be seen as an anarchistic training camp for asymmetrical warfare of the pacifist kind. Its soldiers disperse after a week, subsequently articulating fragments of the farm's enduring mission as undercover agents. Once they are brought back together, a coherence between the films emerges, revealing their initial extraction. The significance of the Film Farm's body of work flows from the dispersion and reunion of the resulting individual works. Individuality and collectivity coincide. Each of the works is made in complete freedom by an artist, and yet the works speak to one another by means of their collective source. When driving through the Canadian countryside, a majority of onlookers would probably not notice anything remarkable when passing Hoffman's farm. But a growing number of films have been made on the premises, each of them revealing an individual way of being there while simultaneously reflecting the wider community of filmmakers. By repeating the same but always differently, the steadily expanding catalogue co-created at the Independent Imaging Retreat reveals diverse aspects of rural life, mediated by the enchanting materiality of photochemical film. The Film Farm's films can be described as a remarkable antidote to the drive for an ever-more-spectacular and dispersed view of the world, as advocated by the mainstream media. Simultaneously, the Film Farm's films give a highly personal insight into the lives of the makers, often radically revealing their divergent sexuality, political orientation, and/or artistic otherness. The Film Farm's films are mostly screened within an experimental film context, and the distribution method is similar to the one used by the makers of *I Love You*. The filmmakers will often travel around with their work, screening selections of shorts in dedicated venues, engaging in discussion with the audience afterward. Although this has a limited reach, the unique quality and content of the films can be fully appreciated and understood in such a context. Spectators are often involved in filmmaking in some capacity: as directors, artists, teachers, or critical thinkers. This specialised audience has the sensibilities to respond to the thoughtfulness, phenomenological experiences, and engaged discussions that these screenings offer.

Kim Knowles's concluding remarks about the Film Farm and affiliated initiatives in *Experimental Film and Photochemical Practices* are significant here: 'To be an artist in the current climate is to frequently find oneself in a situation of precarity' (Knowles, 2020: 177). The community of artists and filmmakers that gathers at the Film Farm is deeply aware of the inexorable problems caused by persistent sexism, racism, colonialism, and ecological decline. The Film Farm functions as an incubator, giving artists breathing space to seek a meaningful artistic response to these social and environmental crises that are spinning out of control. For the duration of the retreat, the participants look for a convergence of more-equal and inclusive social relations and sustainable media practices. As Uri Gordon points out in his article 'Prefigurative Politics between Ethical Practice and Absent Promise', 'activists promoting community sustainability, bioremediation, energy transition and Permaculture system design are among the most attuned to prognoses of collapse' (Gordon, 2017: 29). According to Gordon, a possible strategy to fight off despair is to be found in what he refers to as anxious or catastrophic hope. The Film Farm brings together artists who are 'attuned to prognoses of collapse', not only in terms of the aforementioned crises but also in relation to their medium (photochemical film), branded redundant, or their methodology (artisanal practice), labelled economically marginal. The temporary utopian setting that the

Film Farm offers inserts a dose of positivism into the group. This newfound hope is diffused far beyond the grounds of the retreat.

The structural organisation of a film text based on what Manovich has identified as a database configuration is fitting for the portrayal of a community, a collective, or a habitat, showing a variety of aspects of the main subject in parallel micro-narratives, bringing out their kinship, affinities, commonalities, and contradictions. This can be applied either within the confines of a neighbourhood, a city, or a country, or it can even reach toward a global perspective. Vertov's legacy is enduring and lives on in the hands of many filmmakers, educators, and producers who constantly shape and reinvent his communal agenda. The poetics of the database can be found within rhymes, rhythms, and impromptu patterns emerging from its seemingly random and chaotic input. The examples discussed all use this property, either steered by an expert editor or director or co-created by a group of participants. While the notion of the database is generally understood as being part of the digital domain, the examples demonstrate that the concept can be applied in both digital and analog film productions irrespective of technology. In terms of aesthetics, all examples share a gusto for unpolished images and the deliberate incorporation of technical imperfections. Blurry images, over- and underexposure, scratches and distortions, and digital or chemical accidents are embraced by the filmmakers mentioned above. Moreover, handheld camera work appears in all films, underlining the presence of the filmmaker(s) in the work. In terms of ethics, this chapter has explored prefigurative politics as a guiding principle. Raekstad and Gradin have argued that 'as long as we seek to take power in existing key hierarchical institutions, we will remain stuck in a logic of domination and will not be able to establish a genuinely equal, and democratic society' (Raekstad and Gradin, 2020: 33). It is relevant to consider this argument within the context of the film industry as it is routinely organised in a hierarchical way, following the logic of a top-down approach. The films discussed here explore a bottom-up approach in a number of different ways, either on a quite limited or much more developed scale. In *I Love You*, this combination of crowd-sourced footage and a traditional approach to editing are also applied, but with the clear intention to provide a mouthpiece for the protagonists. The subsequent examples (*The Sound We See* and the films coming out of Film Farm) demonstrate that a comprehensive bottom-up approach is possible and that this method can lead to compelling results. In both examples the participants have collectively agreed on a set of preconditions while continuously sharing and discussing their creative decisions.

Mathijs van de Sande (2020) has pointed out that instead of an electoral-representative form of democracy, prefigurative politics strives for more inclusive forms of participatory democracy. The films discussed in this chapter also explore participation. Each film does this in a distinctive way, demonstrating the limitations and possibilities of such an approach. *I Love You* accomplishes participation in two ways. First, by providing a precise context for the protagonists to shoot their own images in an open dialogue with the directors. Second, by touring the film in a format which encourages discussion between the directors and the audience. This distribution strategy is also employed by the other films considered above. *The Sound We See* involves the contributors not only in shooting the film but in all parts of the production process. This project emphasises participation as a core element, focusing on the process of creation rather than on the final outcome. Finally, the films made during the Independent Imaging Retreat are the result of knowledge exchange, the use of shared resources, and the specificities prescribed by the rural location. A balance is sought between individual liberty and communal interaction. As noted by Holloway, 'we cannot wait for a future that may never come. It is necessary to move beyond now, in the sense of creating a different logic, a different way of talking, a different organisation of doing' (Holloway, 2019: 206). As a medium, cinema is uniquely equipped with the power to evoke new realities. Therefore, it can be a powerful tool for developing such a different logic. Harnessing this power for the progression of a prefigurative agenda is not a simple task, but as demonstrated by the above examples, Vertov's seed has fallen on fertile grounds. The open-ended, experimental nature of prefiguration does not strive for perfection. Instead of making a masterpiece or a blockbuster, the aim here is to create a cultural experience that genuinely involves and inspires people.

9

Multitudes

After commuting between Rotterdam and London for several months, I permanently moved across the channel in 2013. In the Netherlands, experimental film was mostly seen as a thing of the past. In London, the debate around experimental film was much more lively. Enthused by this new climate, I decided to undertake a practice-based research project. In one of the drafts of my research proposal, I wrote that the practical element of my project was going to be an expanded cinema performance in which 'machine, human and space become one living, breathing entity connected with the wider world around it'. One of the first results was the performance *Pattern/Chaos* (2015). I used salt, moss, and grass to make images on expired photochemical film, bringing the ingredients in contact with the emulsion in a number of different ways. Additionally, I made kinetic and shadow objects using found and recuperated materials such as branches, left-over pieces of plywood, and discarded optical glass. These objects were used to break up the film frame, expanding and contracting the image during projection (see figure 9.1). I gathered previously recorded field recordings to create a soundtrack: a waterfall, a forest walk, and a swarm of insects.

In parallel, I had started searching for texts that could help me to underpin my practice with a theoretical framework. I was intrigued by ecologist and philosopher Timothy Morton's book *Ecology without Nature* (Morton, 2007) and not only found a whole new way of thinking about environmentalism and the arts but also stumbled upon the term 'posthumanism' for the first time. Not much later, I found Rosi Braidotti's *The Posthuman* (Braidotti, 2013), which in turn lead me to the writing of Lynn Margulis, Donna Haraway, and Karen Barad. Together, these authors changed my thinking about the natural world profoundly. A particularly important

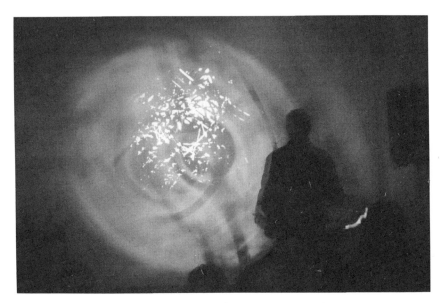

Figure 9.1 *Pattern/Chaos* – Karel Doing (UK 2015, expanded cinema performance, 18min); photograph by Pierre Bouvier Patron.

idea these authors challenge is human exceptionalism. By allowing animals, plants, rocks, and clouds to contribute more actively to the domain that humans call 'culture', a paradigm shift can be achieved. Instead of a humanist point of view in which making meaning is a privilege of *Homo sapiens*, these authors propose a worldview based on an interconnectedness between the natural and the cultural realm.

In many disciplines, the debate about collectivity and individuality is ongoing. Our perception of 'self' leads us to believe that humans are independent beings in control of their own destiny. Consequently, the human species is seen as the pinnacle of evolution. However, the central role of the human subject is increasingly disputed. In the sciences, this discussion has been bolstered by the research of evolutionary biologist Lynn Margulis. One of her major contributions is concerned with the history of life and the evolution of cells. In a groundbreaking article that was published as early as 1967 (under her married name, Lynn Sagan), she proposes that prehistoric free-living bacteria formed symbiotic organisms that paved the way for, and are still included in, more complex life forms such as human beings (Sagan, 1967). Initially her theory was vigorously contested, but her insights are now highly acclaimed and have had an enormous impact on evolutionary biology and other branches of the sciences and the humanities. On the opening page of her book *Symbiotic Planet: A New Look at Evolution*, she writes:

Symbiosis, the system in which members of different species live in physical contact, strikes us as an arcane concept and specialized biological term. This is because of our lack of awareness of its prevalence. Not only are our guts and eyelashes festooned with bacterial and animal symbionts, but if we look at your backyard or community park, symbionts are not obvious but they are omnipresent. (Margulis, 1998: 5)

This 'lack of awareness' still rings true. Few people would be able to name bacterial and animal symbionts, despite their crucial role in nature. Unfortunately, this concept of life as a web of interconnected species is still at odds with a behavioural pattern that is driven by anthropocentrism. To clarify this problem, Margulis emphasises the profound entanglement of life on a global scale:

No matter how much our own species preoccupies us, life is a far wider system. Life is an incredibly complex interdependence of matter and energy among millions of species beyond (and within) our own skin. These Earth aliens are our relatives, our ancestors, and part of us. They cycle our matter and bring us water and food. Without the 'other' we do not survive. Our symbiotic, interactive, interdependent past is connected through animated waters. (Ibid., 111)

This 'interdependence of matter and energy' is best understood when it is connected to our own body and well-being. The study of symbiotic microorganisms that live in our digestive tracts, often referred to as the microbiome, has recently gained in popularity. This is captured in the book *I Contain Multitudes: The Microbes Within Us and a Grander View of Life* (Yong, 2016). Yong challenges the fact that bacteria and fungi are primarily seen as our enemies and proposes an alternative approach:

Say goodbye to the dated and dangerous war metaphors, in which we are soldiers hellbent on eradicating germs at whatever costs. Say hello to a gentler and more nuanced gardening metaphor. Yes, we still have to pull out the weeds, but we also seed and feed species that bind soil, freshen the air, and please the eye. (Ibid., 215)

Microbiota indeed do live in many places: our own bodies, other species including pets and domesticated animals, insects, plants, the soil, and even the air. Complex interactions take place between the different symbiotic partners and the host. These insights lead to a blurring of the boundaries between individual and environment through the introduction of new terminology like 'holobiont': an assemblage of species forming an ecological unit.

Symbiosis is an important source of inspiration for Donna Haraway in her quest to develop a new approach that crosses over between the sciences and the humanities. Trained in both zoology and philosophy, Haraway has published extensively, bringing together primatology, feminism, techno-science, and speculative fiction. She has coined the term 'natureculture', an expression that highlights the profound interconnections between the predominantly separate domains of nature and culture. Furthermore, she has done extensive research in what she calls 'multispecies studies': looking at life through the perspective of an entanglement of species. Her research is focused not only on microbiota but also on the myriad relationships that humans have formed with animals such as dogs, horses, and primates:

To think-with is to stay with the naturalcultural multispecies trouble on earth. There are no guarantees, no arrow of time, no Law of History or Science or Nature in such struggles. There is only the relentlessly contingent SF worlding of living and dying, of becoming-with and unbecoming-with, of sympoiesis, and so, just possibly, of multispecies flourishing on earth. (Haraway, 2016: 40)

Margulis's insights into symbiosis and Haraway's multispecies studies have contributed to a wider critical rethinking of our relationship with the biosphere. Inevitably, this line of enquiry has also reached further afield, beyond organic lifeforms. As global heating, ocean acidification, and soil erosion show us, life on earth exists in a feedback loop with the atmosphere, the oceans, and the soil. Timothy Morton comments wittily:

We expect rocks to play their part, which is to say, be totally passive. We're the top, they're the bottom and we expect them to stay that way. When they play at being on top, humans call it an earthquake and find it highly unpleasant. Or, consider a rock falling on one's car: there are road hazard signs showing how it happens, but we never read those signs as if rocks somehow jump off the cliff and hurtle toward us. We are hampered even from the beginning to ascribe intention to rocks, the issue that lurks in the background of the notion of agency. (Morton, 2017: 180)

Morton continues by observing that 'a rock is a gigantic empty cathedral at a microscopic level; at nanoscopic level it is a vast empty region of a solar system' (ibid., 186–187). Conversely, he also considers a magnified perspective on the subject: 'On an inhumanly large timescale, rocks behave like liquids, coming and going, moving, shifting, melting. Rocks fail to sit still there doing nothing' (ibid., 187). In *The Discovery of Slowness* (Nadolny, 2004), a fictionalised biography of Arctic explorer John Franklin, the central character of the book discovers how his particular slowness can be an advantage. Through precise and sustained observation, he is able to see the gradual changes in weather, landscape, wave patterns in water, and the movement of celestial bodies. Franklin understands the timescale of meteorological and cosmological events and even imagines himself turning into a stone, extending his range to geological time. Instead of being cast out as a 'retard', the hero embarks on a stellar career as a navigator, taking advantage of his unprecedented ability to foresee changes in the weather. A fellow seaman describes him aptly by commenting that 'he never loses time' (ibid., 85), an interesting refutation of the prevalent interpretation of 'losing time'. According to this alternative reading, acting quickly can be seen to lead to an increased chance of misinterpretation as it glosses over the slower processes that affect the planet.

The idea that inert objects like rocks can have a more active presence than generally assumed is underpinned by Karen Barad's theory of 'agential realism'. Barad is trained as a theoretical physicist and has extended her research into the domain of philosophy and feminist theory. In her influential book *Meeting the Universe Halfway* (Barad, 2007), she uses a practice of science-based approach to examine the concept of scientific objectivity. Even though she doesn't leave out the complexity of quantum theory, her hands-on approach makes her book accessible to a broad audience. After a thorough investigation of many different concepts in this field, consistently underpinned by descriptions of experiments and analyses of the results, she concludes with a number of propositions, suggesting a new way of looking at objectivity. She writes that 'according to quantum field theory, the vacuum is far from empty: indeed, it's teeming with the full set of possibilities of what may come to be' (ibid., 354). The implication of such an emergent view on reality is that 'objectivity is a matter of accountability for what materializes' (ibid., 361). In other words, objectivity is not a fixed state of things that exists outside of us but rather a dynamic state that both responds to and interrogates our perception. She concludes that '*embodiment is a matter not of being specifically situated in the world, but rather of being in the world in its dynamic specificity*' (ibid., 377, emphasis in original). Such an embodied form of 'being in the world in its dynamic specificity' invites us to acknowledge the pervasiveness of natural phenomena such as electricity, magnetism, radioactivity, and all the mysterious events that occur on quantum levels. From this point of view, the border between the inside and the outside of the body vanishes, and the universe appears as a borderless expanse of interconnected events.

Such new directions in thinking about the relation between ourselves and the natural world are also reflected in the work of experimental filmmakers. The interaction between body, microbiota, and environment is concretely and imaginatively visualised by experimental filmmaker Louise Bourque in her film *Jours en Fleurs* (2003). To make her film, the artist applied menstrual fluids to 35mm footage of flowering trees. The result is a layering of seemingly abstract colours and textures that alternate and coincide with the barely persisting images of branches and flowers (see figure 9.2). The blooming trees are obscured, almost nocturnal in their presence. Thick accumulations of blood and uterine cells have created dark blooms on the emulsion, surrounded by a deep red haze. The thinner

Figure 9.2 *Jours en Fleurs* – Louise Bourque (CA 2003, 16mm film, colour, 5min); courtesy of Lightcone.

streaks of menstrual fluid provide a more granular, earthy red-brown texture, reminiscent of soil. Cracks in the film's emulsion add green, purple, and yellow notes to the colour palette. The colourful specks could be mistaken for flowers, briefly brightening up the dark environs. The images pulsate rhythmically in sync with the spectator's breathing and heartbeat. On the soundtrack, sounds of birds and rustling trees are combined with a noisy background that calls to mind the interior of the body, like the rushing of blood and lymph through the circulatory system. Bourque blurs the boundaries between interior and exterior in her film, first of all by bringing the menstrual fluids literally in contact with images of blossoming trees. But beyond this performative action, the images and sounds relay a haunting presence that crosses over between interior apprehension and exterior menace. In her next film, *L'Éclat du Mal / The Bleeding Heart of It* (2005), this feeling of being haunted both internally and externally is made more explicit by means of a gritty voice-over: 'In my dream there's a war going on. It's Christmas time. I'm running and I'm carrying myself as a child. It's dark in the tunnel and I'm heading towards the light, the daylight' (Tribeca Festival, 2020). Again, abstract patterns and colours are layered with camera footage, this time with images of a house and what appears to be family portraits. Halfway through the film, the rhythm changes from slow and dreamy to fast and disturbing. The whistle and boom of falling and detonating bombs can be heard. After this brief intermission, the film returns to a slower pace but maintains its ghostly character. The anguished cry of a bird finds its way into the soundtrack, coinciding dramatically with the distorted voice and the sinister synthesiser sounds. Both films allow the image to become permeable, threatening disintegration and loss of legibility but also setting in motion a transformation. *Jours en Fleurs*, with its explicit reference to menstrual blood and vaginal microbiota, transforms something that 'has been codified as something uncontrollable that needs to be organised, managed, and contained (Green-Cole, 2020: 788) into a darkly beautiful and challengingly disobedient experience. In conversation with Micah Malone, Bourque comments on the title of her film: 'It has a certain loveliness to it but also a certain violence, the idea that you can't say you have a period, because of the taboo' (Malone, 2021: 123). Furthermore, she states that 'the film captures both the beauty of nature and its destructive force' (ibid.). This brings us back to Yong's comments about microbiota and the supposed opposition between war and gardening metaphors. Arguably, both can be apt. The relation between the human body and its microbiota can be described as a battlefield and a thriving community at the same time. Life and death, symbiosis and infection, are only separated by a hair's breadth. Bourque concludes by simply saying: 'There's always blood at birth' (ibid.).

In *It Matters What* (2019), Canadian experimental filmmaker Franci Duran incorporates fragments of Haraway's essay 'Tentacular Thinking: Anthropocene, Capitalocene, Chthulucene' (Haraway, 2016). Duran has chosen a hybrid and layered approach, combining analog and digital media, new and found footage. She superimposes these images, and the film oscillates between the realistic and the abstract. Shots are rehashed using a variety of scales and tempi. Scratches and particles dance across the screen, partially obscuring the image. The text fragments appear both in a voice-over (read by a child) and in animated letters attached to a filmstrip. At first, the animation allows the spectator to read the text, but in subsequent variations the animation is too fast to be legible. In both cases, meaning emerges and breaks down, evoking a feeling of impermanence. In the first half of the film, a key scene shows a woman holding a dead owl; she is spreading its wings, smiling cunningly to the camera (see figure 9.3). This image is repeated again and again, allowing different readings through

Figure 9.3 *It Matters What* – Francisca Duran (CA 2019, HD video, colour & bw, 9min); courtesy of the artist.

reframing and recombining the image with different layers of more abstract imagery. Astonishment is followed by disgust with the gratuitous manipulation of the animal's dead body, and is then overridden again by admiration for the majestic bird. Duran's thoughtful use of this shot brings to mind the words of Chickasaw writer and environmentalist Linda Hogan: 'For years I prayed for an eagle feather. I wanted one from a bird still living. A killed eagle would offer me none of what I hoped for. A bird killed in the name of human power is in truth a loss of power from the world, not an addition to it' (Hogan, 1995: 15). At the end of the sequence, the child's voice and the animated text re-emerge out of the granular and hypnotic drone that forms the basic layer of the soundtrack. Instead of the ambiguous opening words, the text now directly confronts the spectator with the anxiety and shock caused by climate change and species extinction:

These times called the Anthropocene are times of multispecies, including human, urgency: of great mass death and extinction; of onrushing disasters, whose unpredictable specificities are foolishly taken as unknowability itself; of refusing to know and to cultivate the capacity of response-ability; of refusing to be present in and to onrushing catastrophe in time; of unprecedented looking away. (Haraway, 2016: 35)

It is not only the woman with the dead owl who is called out, but also we, the spectators. The second half of the film consists of animated phytograms, visible traces rendered directly on the filmstrip by means of phytochemistry and sunlight (see chapter 11). The film answers to its environment, attempting to materialise a form of Haraway's desired response-ability. The scratch marks and granular degradation of the film's emulsion remind the spectator of the impermanence of bodies and objects. The phytographic sequence evokes a world that is alive and radiant. Life and death, degradation and growth walk hand in hand. But the tipping point is precariously close. Duran carefully arranges the spectator's experience, aiming to draw their attention to the perilous slow-motion crash of the biosphere.

Before the advent of environmentalism, posthumanism, and multispecies studies, the evolutionary biologist Charles Darwin already paved the way for a different way of thinking about *Homo sapiens*:

As monkeys certainly understand much that is said to them by man, and as in a state of nature they utter signal-cries of danger to their fellows, it does not appear altogether incredible, that some unusually wise ape-like animal should have thought of imitating the growl of a beast of prey, so as to indicate to his fellow monkeys the nature of the expected danger. And this would have been a first step in the formation of a language. (Darwin, 1981: 57)

The relationship between humans and monkeys and their respective intelligence is explored by American experimental filmmaker Eve Heller in her found-footage film *Last Lost* (1996). The film offers a Freudian point of view, setting the tone in the opening shots, juxtaposing a lone chimpanzee and a crowd of people bathing and playing in the sea at the amusement park at Coney Island Beach. The chimp cuddles intimately with a bikini-clad woman while the anonymous crowd leisurely bobs in the waves. The relation between the chimpanzee and the woman gradually develops throughout the film in a suggestive and ambiguous way, with the completion of the narrative taking place in the mind of the spectator (see figure 9.4). The chimpanzee climbs on the roller coaster and takes a ride hanging on one of the attractions in the amusement park while the

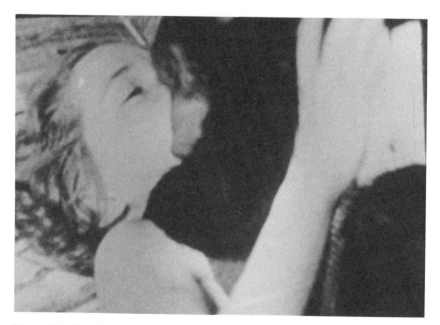

Figure 9.4 *Last Lost* – Eve Heller (US 1996, 16mm film, bw, 14min); courtesy of the artist.

woman is taking part in a beauty contest. Her waist is measured, and she lines up with other women. Suddenly she faints, the chimpanzee carries a glass bottle and climbs high onto the roller coaster. A brief shot reveals the label 'Ammonium Carbonate' on a similar glass bottle; another shot shows the woman waking up after smelling the bottle, while the chimpanzee sits next to her. Recurrent shots are reframed by zooming in and slowing down the original footage. Images appear that are just a few frames long, registering only subliminally. The crowd keeps churning, joking, and laughing. The woman seems to be the only person who has a more tender and friendly relationship with the chimpanzee but she also takes part in the summer vacation activities at the seaside. The chimpanzee is portrayed in a more detached way, seemingly melancholic but also purposeful and serious in his actions. Unconventionally, an animal here takes on the role of the protagonist. In a videotaped interview with Xcèntric (Xcèntric, 2009), a cinema which is part of the Centre of Contemporary Culture in Barcelona, Heller states: 'I tried to make instead the figure of the chimpanzee a witness to the strange human universe.' The strangeness of human behaviour is emphasised by Heller's deliberate anthropomorphising of the chimpanzee. Simultaneously, the spectator is aware that the film is based on pre-existing footage which is edited and rephotographed to create a different point of view from that of the original film. A presumably secure human-animal hierarchy suddenly wavers, with the animal being the more thoughtful and responsible character. Even in the end credits of the film, the order of things is destabilised by means of a reverse shot. A wave pulls back, magically revealing an inscription written on the beach. *Last Lost* comments on an all-too-human world through the eyes of the chimpanzee, offering a melancholic but simultaneously refreshing view on interspecies relationships.

A precise and sustained observation of rocks, water, and weather can be found in the films of the late David Dudouit, a French experimental filmmaker who focused on shooting frame by frame over prolonged periods of time, covering hours and even days. His film *Cailloux, Roches, Algues* (2009) is shot on the remote Breton island Île de Sein. The grainy black-and-white Super 8 images interact with the roughness of the landscape, the choppiness of the waves, and the fog that drifts in and out. The low resolution of the image steers the spectator's attention toward the grander patterns that occur in time. Instead of the commonly used advanced technological representation of landscape in nature documentaries, Dudouit's film presents us with an observational challenge. Realism does not translate into perfection here. Instead, the film offers a phenomenological experience: a 'being there' rather than a 'looking at'. It is as if our ocular cilia, the sensory antennae in the eye (see further May-Simera, Nagel-Wolfrum & Wolfrum, 2017), can touch the cold, smooth roundness of the pebbles on the beach, the rugged surface of the weathered rocks, and the damp mantle of the incoming fog. Each of the three sequences the film comprises is composed 'in camera' in a process that involves an intense observation of landscape and weather combined with a profound knowledge of the cinematic apparatus. There is no editing or other post-production besides the enlargement of the fragile Super 8 film onto 16mm internegative and projection print. This lack of interference subverts the spectator's expectation of cinema as a narrative medium while offering a glimpse into a world inhabited by more-than-human entities such as rocks and oceans.

Vicky Smith dives into the world of matter on a microscopic or perhaps even nanoscopic level. In her film *Small Things Moving in Unison* (2018), tiny pinpricks turn into particles moving in ways that are both randomised and organised. The individual dots never appear in exactly the same position as in the previous frame. Neither do they move into a particular direction. However, collections of dots are brought together in constantly changing fields. The film opens with such a field emerging from the left and bulging out elliptically until the whole frame is covered. After a few seconds of Brownian movement, the field collapses into a decreasing band. When only a handful of dots remain, their movement appears more wavelike. The dots swell in number and again cover the whole screen before turning into an egg-like shape. A round hole appears in the egg, pushing the entire shape toward the edges of the frame. A further succession of shapes grows out of the random Brownian motion of the individual dots. Changes in size result in an illusion of movement, protruding outward, sinking back, going right, left, up, and down. In a final sequence, the dots themselves grow in size, culminating into rougher jagged shapes with torn edges. These shapes again diminish in size, and the total number of dots decreases until the screen is empty. On the soundtrack, Shirley Pegna uses her voice to create speech-like sounds close to breathing, whistling, rolling, and clicking. No words are formed, but meaning is just around the corner, especially in conjunction with the image. Possibly, we are witnessing the firing of neurones, the decryption of a process, the formation of a signal out of chaos. The tiny pinpricks spring to life and become entangled, like Barad's quantum particles that emerge from a vacuum. Such intra-actions (to use Barad's terminology) between light, energy, matter, and the biosphere are a recurring theme in Smith's work, as exemplified by her films *Primal* (2017), in which colours flicker like a flame, and *Not (A) Part* (2019), a film that focuses on the wings, legs, thorax, head, and antennae of dead bees. In an article about this last film, the filmmaker clarifies her process and highlights the significance of the mixture of organic and non-organic materials that she has used:

The film was shaped by process and encounters, themselves the heart of much creative practice research, and these contingencies contributed to the project's originality. The urgency and scale of the issue of insect extinction is communicated by an aesthetic style that had not been originally intended: for example that of the superimposed wings, not flying, but tumbling en masse and without direction. [...] Things mingle in the depthless and opaque ground, yet their individual properties are pronounced in terms of how they move in relation to the film: large grains mixing with fine crystals create depth cues, particles of skin float to the top, furry bits hover, long wing and leg shapes spin, strands of hair and pins travel lengthways cutting across frames, while propolis oozes in a downward direction. (Smith, 2019)

The common factor in the films of Bourque, Duran, Heller, Dudouit, and Smith is that the artists are interested in a more-than-human point of view: organic matter comes into contact with the filmstrip, animals become protagonists, background becomes foreground, time is compressed in order to reveal meteorological events, materiality transforms into energy and vice versa. Each in their own way, these films are inquiries into the 'nature of nature' and the 'future of nature', intersecting with the theories of Margulis, Haraway, Morton, and Barad. Duran explicitly references Haraway by integrating a text citation in her film *It Matters What*. The other examples demonstrate how topics such as human-animal relations, the biosphere as a dynamic system, the agency of matter and energy, and species extinction have become much more pronounced within the arts in general and experimental film in particular. Taken together, these films can be bracketed under the umbrella term 'posthumanism'. There are many more experimental filmmakers that can also be mentioned in this context: Anna Kipervaser, Kelly Egan, Caryn Cline, Robert Schaller, Peter Conrad-Beyer, and others.

However, 'posthumanism' can be deceptive as a term, especially within the context of the media arts. The 'post' in 'posthumanism' frequently refers to a shift in our relationship with machines. The same issue is also central to transhumanist thinking. But contrary to the critical stance of contemporary posthumanists, transhuman thinkers are much more inclined to fast-forward toward a disembodied future. In her groundbreaking essay 'A Cyborg Manifesto', the leading posthuman thinker Donna Haraway asserts that 'by the late twentieth century, our time, a mythic time, we are all chimeras, theorized and fabricated hybrids of machine and organism – in short, cyborgs' (Haraway, 1991: 150). The new human/machine relation is an intimate one. However, Haraway's mention of intimacy points toward a critical form of posthumanism that is focused not merely on machines and digital technology but also on the human body. A body that is simultaneously human, animal, and machine. A body that is as much part of the biosphere as it is part of the technosphere. To go back to Haraway: 'The cyborg appears in myth precisely where the boundary between human and animal is transgressed. Far from signalling a walling off of people from other living beings, cyborgs signal disturbingly and pleasurably tight coupling' (Ibid., 152). Such a 'disturbingly and pleasurably tight coupling' is reflected in the work of the above-discussed experimental filmmakers via sensuous explorations of the materiality of the medium and the subject matter. Surface damage, chemical intra-action, film grain, slow motion, time lapse, and mark making are all used to connect – rather than separate – internal and external modes of awareness. The owl, the plants, the chimp, the rocks, and the dots are given prominent roles within the respective films, acting on a plane that is usually reserved for human protagonists.

An important comment within this context can be found in the influential book *The Posthuman* by philosopher Rosi Braidotti: 'Humans have spread to non-humans their fundamental anxiety about the future' (Braidotti, 2013: 79). To counteract such a mindset, she proposes an 'eco-philosophy of multiple belongings' that is 'based on a strong sense of collectivity, relationality and hence community building' (ibid., 49). As there is no functioning language that works across species, and there certainly is no cinematic language that can take on such a role, attempts to configure such cinematic narratives are necessarily humble and incomplete. I like to think of these films as an alternative to science fiction; instead of spaceships and gleaming skyscrapers, there is a focus on an evolved form of social relationships. It takes imagination to look at earth and its ruined biosphere and still anticipate the birth of a new form of communication, a meaningful dialogue that involves more of those profoundly alien creatures, hard-to-grasp global events, and presumably inert objects and materials that coexist on this small planet. The material of film is not only made the subject of the interrogation but is objectively and semiotically intertwined with those other lives that should be listened to in the pandemonium known as the Anthropocene.

10

Naturefuture

His eyes are staring, his mouth is open, his wings are spread. This is how one pictures the angel of history. His face is turned toward the past. Where we perceive a chain of events, he sees one single catastrophe which keeps piling wreckage upon wreckage and hurls it in front of his feet. The angel would like to stay, awaken the dead, and make whole what has been smashed. But a storm is blowing from Paradise; it has got caught in his wings with such violence that the angel can no longer close them. This storm irresistibly propels him into the future to which his back is turned, while the pile of debris before him grows skyward. This storm is what we call progress. (Benjamin, 2007: 257)

Walter Benjamin wrote these words shortly before he committed suicide in order to avoid being captured by the Gestapo. Benjamin's essay is a reflection on human history, specifically the historical events that robbed him and so many others of their lives. His words make tangible the terror of persecution and genocide. This terror is felt not only by the victims of such violence but also by survivors and witnesses. The 'pile of debris' mentioned by Benjamin is visible to anyone who does not turn their head away.

Between 2008 and 2010, I made a series of journeys to Suriname, a Dutch-speaking country part of the Guiana region in South America. My aim was to find out more about the autonomous communities living along the upper Suriname River: the Saamaka or Saramaka. The Saamaka are the descendants of enslaved people who liberated themselves, building an entirely new society on the South American continent after being ripped away from their African roots. After my first – only partially successful – journey, I met the unforgettable cultural activist Humphrey Schmidt in my hometown of Rotterdam. He introduced me to the artist collective Totomboti (Woodpeckers), based in the village Pikin Slee. We established contact and collaborated on two film projects: the experimental 16mm film *Looking for Apoekoe* (2010) and the archive-based documentary *Saamaka*

(2010). The first film is a visual exploration of the bush spirit Apoekoe or Apuku, a mythical figure with complex characteristics, similar to the Greek god Pan. The second film is a reworking of a colonial film about the burial of a *granman* (chieftain). Through the addition of a soundtrack composed of comments, parables, music, and sounds brought together by the people of Pikin Slee, the footage is given back to the Saamaka people. These projects brought the enduring problematic legacy of colonialism and slavery into sharp relief. My films divided the audience: on the one side, my efforts were denounced as irrelevant, and on the other side, they were seen as essential. If one thing became clear, it was the fact that the discussion about slavery and the involvement of the Netherlands in this dehumanising practice was far from finished. Upon being confronted with the polarised reactions of the audience, I found Benjamin's pile of debris more concrete than I had realised before travelling westwards. Johan Lau Munkholm makes a similar connection, reflecting on the narrator and main character (Data Thief) in the pivotal Afrofuturist film *The Last Angel of History* by John Akomfrah (1996):

Considering the progressive accumulation of wealth produced on the backs of slaves during colonialism, the lasting wounds it afflicted on generations of descendants, and the general forgetfulness that surrounds this process in the West, Benjamin's critique of historicism resonates forcefully today. The legacy the Data Thief has inherited from Benjamin is a quest to destroy this continuum. To do this, it is vital to recognize that historical causality is constructed retrospectively and that any construction can be upset. (Munkholm, 2018: 53)

Akomfrah's film seeks to examine the trauma of the Middle Passage, the forced and often lethal voyage of enslaved Africans across the Atlantic. As Kodwo Eshun writes in his article 'Further Considerations on Afrofuturism', 'instead of civilizing African subjects, the forced dislocation and commodification that constituted the Middle Passage meant that modernity was rendered forever suspect' (Eshwun, 2003: 288). Eswhun argues that the Euro-American slave trade has resulted in a profound alienation of its victims. If we rethink the theme of abduction and forced relocation to another territory/planet, a subject matter frequently found in science fiction, this motif suddenly becomes nonfictional. As a result, Afrofuturism was already a reality before the term was coined. Such a revelatory entanglement between fiction and nonfiction unfolds in *The Last Angel of History*. In the opening sequence, a narrator introduces us to a secret Black technology; the Blues. He is standing in a flooded and barren landscape and reappears throughout the film in similar locations. Derelict buildings, wrecked cars, and discarded technology feature in these shots. This is the Data Thief: an imaginary character from the future who pursues the decoding of the aforementioned secret technology. The Data Thief wears a futuristic version of Inuit protective eyewear. Throughout the film, short animated sequences are inserted that combine images of African cultural artefacts, mathematical symbols, civil rights–era photos, space-age technology, and geometrical forms. The footage is predominantly tinted in bright orange and blue colours. Sometimes the image is split or layered, and often a computer screen appears in the image. On the soundtrack, this approach is extended with the inclusion of fragments of blues, jazz, funk, and techno music, alongside electronic sound effects. The different styles of music are discussed in the film. Past, present, and future are commingled in such a way that the spectator's chronology is thrown into doubt. The film thus reimagines both the past and the future. The importance of this strategy is underlined by Eshwun: 'African social reality is overdetermined by intimidating global scenarios, doomsday economic projections, weather predictions, medical reports on AIDS, and life-expectancy forecasts, all of which predict decades of immiserization' (ibid., 292). Within this context of negative predictions, it has become virtually impossible to imagine a hopeful future for the diverse countries that constitute the African continent. This effect contributes to the general low esteem that African culture is met with. Eshwun continues: 'Afrofuturism, then, is concerned with the possibilities for intervention within the dimension of the predictive, the projected, the proleptic, the envisioned, the virtual, the anticipatory and the future conditional' (ibid., 293). This makes clear that Afrofuturism is a methodology, not just a style. A similar approach can be used in other contexts as well, such as the genocide of Indigenous people of the Americas and the subsequent and ongoing violations of their civil and human rights. The films of the Indigenous North and South American artists Sky Hopinka and Colectivo Los Ingrávidos (Collective of the Weightless) interfere with a predictive cultural framework as well, counteracting the prevalent negative framing of Indigenous Americans.

Hopinka situates his own work within a broad First Nations context, specifically centred on his own frame of reference as a Ho-Chunk national and descendent of the Pechanga Band of Luiseño Indians. Recurrent motifs in his work are language, landscape, and a circular and poetic form of storytelling. In a conversation between five artists about film and language, Hopinka comments on the use of English alongside pidgin and Indigenous languages in his films: 'I won't look at these communities as victims of a broken system, but rather as groups of people that have adapted and shaped this language for their own purposes, survival, representations of culture in spite of those colonial acts' (Sachs et al., 2018). In a further interview, published in *A Companion to Experimental Cinema*, he highlights the importance of *The Exiles* (Mackenzie, 1961), a film that chronicles the lives of a group of young Indigenous Americans, as a formative influence on his own work:

It was something that gave me permission as a Native person growing up in the U.S. to not follow prescribed modes of storytelling that are about overcoming the victimization that we've experienced and rather makes a space for culture and then allows the culture and community to fill that space out. (Fox, 2018)

Both statements make clear that he uses a radical 'being in the present' as a point of departure. In his short experimental film *Jáaji Approx*, he uses recordings of his father, who is talking and singing in a mix of American English and Indigenous language. This might seem to contradict the notion of a 'present tense', but Hopinka responds to the recordings in the present tense. Speech acts are connected with footage of landscapes in a poetic way, resulting in the formation of new vantage points. On the title card, the Hočak word *Jáaji* is translated as 'Father (direct address)', making clear that this is an active response rather than an effort to present an archive. The opening shot is taken from the front window of a car. Only a few other cars are visible in the distance. On the horizon, a moss-green mountain range is visible. Above this mountain range, much taller, snow-covered mountains seem to hover in the sky. The accompanying voice on the soundtrack establishes the date and time: April 16, 2007, 2.45 p.m. In the second shot, the same snow-covered mountains appear upside-down. A beep accentuates the splice between the shots. Words appear written phonetically in the middle of the screen, while also being spoken: 'the dreaming, the time, even the beat'. Taken together, these two shots are representative of the film's experimental intertwining of documentary, ethnographic, and poetic elements. The following sequence is predominantly taken with a handheld camera, with the film-maker roaming through the land on foot. Casually; but still shot in a precise manner. The handheld sequence is punctuated by a shot of a busy highway taken from the front window of a car. The voice makes us aware that the function of singing songs is 'to make the dancers dance'. A second date and time is introduced with an almost black frame: December 13, 2005. Only the reflected light of a car's indicator is faintly visible on a white line on the side of a road. The voice switches from talking to singing, until a truck drives past, sweeping the frame and soundtrack with its noisy combustion engine and glaring headlights. Further singing is accompanied by shots of bright summer clouds and mountains that appear simultaneously at the top and at the bottom of the frame. In the final sequence, the recording of a travelling song is answered with further superimpositions. Instead of documentary representations of landscape, these compositions are closer to a form of visual music, drawing attention to colour, movement, and texture. The penultimate shot takes the spectator across a suspension bridge illuminated against the night (figure 10.1). The cables form a pattern across a divide. In the final shot, a person appears, thoughtfully looking out of the window of a car. Is this the filmmaker or his father?

Figure 10.1 *Jáaji Approx* – Sky Hopinka (US 2015, HD video, colour, 7min); courtesy of the artist.

As noted by the American ecologist and philosopher David Abram, Indigenous Americans have a deeply felt relationship with the land:

Particular mountains, canyons, streams, boulder-strewn fields, or groves of trees have not yet lost the expressive potency and dynamism with which they spontaneously present themselves to the senses. A particular place in the land is never, for an oral culture, just a passive or inert setting for the human events that occur there. It is an active participant in those occurrences. (Abram, 1997: 162)

In his film *Jáaji Approx* (2015), Hopinka relates to this oral culture by connecting the recorded stories and music with images of the land. Strikingly, he does not select images of wilderness or unspoiled landscapes, which would be typically associated with Indigenous culture. Instead, he chooses a variety of different shots of the land, representing both natural beauty and modernity. By means of framing and editing, he achieves a particular 'expressive potency and dynamism'. Throughout his film, there is a sense of belonging that does not stop at the borders of the reservation and instead stretches out across the land. In parallel, his moving images are skilfully incorporated within the oral tradition, making the work enticing for a contemporary audience – not only Hopinka's own community but also a wider public, particularly a viewership attuned to experimental film. The film's superimpositions, associative editing techniques, phenomenological effects, and bright colours are carefully applied in order to bring the cultural knowledge contained in the audio recordings into the present and into the spectator's frame of reference. Again, David Abram provides a thoughtful analogy here:

When I allow the past and the future to dissolve, imaginatively, into the immediacy of the present moment, then the 'present' itself expands to become an enveloping field of presence. And this presence, vibrant and alive, spontaneously assumes the precise shape and contour of the enveloping sensory landscape, as though this were its native shape! (Ibid., 202–203)

This is where Hopinka's praxis intersects with Afrofuturism. Instead of following 'prescribed modes of storytelling', the filmmaker occupies a space and a medium designed by and for modernism and bends these into his own direction. The 'future conditional' is not always in need of spacecrafts but can simply come to life by evoking a discrete sense of the present that answers to Indigenous culture.

In addition to creating his own work and teaching film and electronic arts at Bard College, Hopinka has also co-founded a platform for indigenous artists: COUSIN, which includes the previously mentioned Colectivo Los Ingrávidos. Colectivo Los Ingrávidos was formed in Tehuacán, Mexico, in 2012. Their name is taken from a novel by Valeria Luiselli in which she intertwines two narrators who both become increasingly detached and wander like ghosts through their respective environments – Mexico City and New York. 'Los Ingrávidos' translates into English as 'the weightless' or 'those unaffected by the force of gravity'. Researcher and filmmaker Raquel Schefer summarises their work in the following way:

Los Ingrávidos has produced a counter-hegemonic cinema addressing the effects of narco-neoliberalism, gendered violence, and femicide. Its films also explore the possibility of creating different methods of perceiving and cognition in line with the early twentieth-century avant-garde theories. It emphasizes the capacity of cinema to restore the experience of ritual and the sacred, suppressed by modern rationality, and therefore to re-enchant the world. (Schefer, 2022)

In their sixty-one minute long cycle *The Sun Quartet* (2017), all of the above is present. The film was shot on expired 16mm colour negative that was processed by hand. Fading colours and blemishes give the film a battered and bruised look, while the speed and intensity of the images invoke a spirit of resilience and vitality. References can be found to both the 1968 Tlatelolco massacre and the 2014 disappearance of forty-three students in Iguala, but the film digs much deeper into the violence and genocide the Indigenous people of Mexico have suffered for centuries. Recurrent images of a ruined regional school and *maquila*, a sweatshop situated in one of Mexico's 'free trade' zones, appear in the context of class and gender struggles – the school being a place where peasants could find education, and the *maquila* being the workplace of a predominantly female workforce. By means of superimposition, in-camera editing, swooping camera movements, and circular and repetitive elements, the film induces a trance-like experience in the mind and body of the spectator. The first section of the quartet is titled *Piedra de Sol*, or Sunstone, in reference to the Aztec calendar stone that was unearthed in 1790, lying face down in the Plaza Meyor of Mexico City. In traditional scholarship, it is assumed that the central character depicted on the stone represents the daytime sun, the deity Tonatiuh. Art historian Cecilia F. Klein argues that the Aztecs divided both space and time into segments corresponding to the five world directions and arranged them in a cyclic sequence that ran east, north, west, south, and center. The east and north were associated with sunrise and noon, and thus the sky by day; the west, south, and center were associated with sunset and midnight, the night sky, the earth, and death. The south and center in particular were associated with the precise moment of midnight and the underworld; it was at this time and in these regions that all Postclassic cosmic cycles came to an end. (Klein, 1976: 2–3)

The film does not follow any particular theory or religious dogma but unapologetically concatenates Aztec, Christian, Marxist, and modernist signs and symbols. Abundance, the sacred, rebirth, love, and passion are symbolised by watermelons, maize, cactuses, roses, and dahlias. The sun shines brightly throughout most of the film, sometimes directly into the camera, burning the image with its white light. Death and violence creep into the film with images of a ruined school, protesting students and farmers, scorched fields, and leaking flames (see figure 10.2). Punctures in the film's material appear briefly as black haloed dots on a white background.

Figure 10.2 *The Sun Quartet* – Colectivo Los Ingrávidos (MX 2017, 16mm film, colour, 61min); courtesy of the artists.

A jazzy improvised soundtrack creates a moody atmosphere, before gradually becoming more feverish. Creative and destructive forces intermingle in this opening piece. The second part is longer and takes the spectator into the heart of the protest against the government's neglect and denial in regard to the case of the missing students. The soundtrack consists of a call and answer between an amplified voice and the many voices in the crowd:

> The call-and-response turns to that haunting demand: 'because they took them alive / we want them back alive.' As the protestors count to 43, the dense images assume the metaphor of the river, a river of mourning and outraged faces, government buildings and a distant moon crossing the flesh of fruit and the needles of cacti. (Broomer, 2023: 11)

Images of the marching demonstrators and their gathering on the central square are superimposed with shots from the countryside and the life-giving produce that the earth offers. The mother of one of the disappeared students gives a powerful speech. In the third part, David Huerta's poem 'Ayotzinapa' (2014) is recited in Chinese, immediately placing the victims of state violence in a global context. Images of gleaming skyscrapers, workers on the field, the window of the school, ripening corn, the sun, traffic at night, and flaring flames oscillate on the screen. Exploding tear gas grenades can be heard while the riot police requests that the protesters abstain from violence. The crowd keeps chanting and singing in defiance of brutal repression. In part 4, the focus shifts toward commemorations in which Christian symbols such as candles and angels appear together with Indigenous emblems. Huerta's poem is read out in multiple languages, providing a more meditative cadence to this twenty-two-minute segment, the longest of the quartet.

There is a similarity between the Indigenous present tense that Hopinka establishes in his work and the 'speculative realism' that underpins *The Sun Quartet*. The images and sounds recorded by the collective during demonstrations against the violent narco-state are brutally real. By combining this straightforward documentary footage with an excessive amount of superimposed layers, *The Sun Quartet* takes the 'real' into another realm. Remarkably, none of the additional layers actually contain fictional or otherwise non-documentary elements. Instead, different planes are brought into contact with each other, disrupting the spectator's concept of the real. Divisions such as countryside vs urban, human vs other-than-human, Hispanic vs Indigenous, and literal vs symbolic are dissolved into a trance-inducing pulse of light and sound that deliberately hinders the spectator from separating these elements. Simultaneously, a linear concept of time is abolished in favour of a cyclical temporality. The film not only links the Tlatelolco massacre with the disappearance of forty-three students in 2014 but situates these events within a much broader history of violence and genocide. While the Aztec *Piedra del Sol* or Sunstone does not appear in the film, its complex mythical presence and postcolonial significance is reflected in the film's composition and materiality. Title and intertitles, poetry, chants, placards, vegetables and flowers, buildings, and symbols all have traceable meanings that are brought together into a new reality that refuses to differentiate between discrete periods in history. An elaboration can be found in the collective's manifesto on the audiovisual:

Shamanic Materialism proceeds by fragments, ruptures, loops, clusters, modules, drifts, ascents, descents, series, spirals, vortexes, pulses, rhythms, entropy, negentropy, hypostasis, collisions, linkages, aberrations, folds, burials, unearthings; and everything which reveals intermittent constellations and from whose magma figures, agitations, forms, structures, processes, relationships, perceptions, speculations and sensations emerge. Shamanic Materialism is a Mesoamerican spell unleashed. (Colectivo Los Ingrávidos, 2022: 188)

This conjunction of ancient (shamanism) and modern (materialism) concepts leads back to Eshwun's methodological examination of Afrofuturism and Benjamin's historical materialism. Instead of taking the backseat in history, Meso-American culture is re-established as a powerful force. *The Sun Quartet*'s 'future conditional' summons a Mexican reality that is simultaneously modern and ancient, making possible a future in which shamanic practices are understood as much more than merely archaic rituals. Eduardo Viveiros de Castro's concept 'multinaturalism' is helpful for exploring this further: in contrast to Western multiculturalism, this philosophy of life presupposes a unity of mind and a diversity of bodies. Mind, in the particular case of *The Sun Quartet*, is distributed among the people, the missing students, the cactuses, the maize, the ruins of the school and workshop, the film material itself, and the sun. The connection between cinema and shamanism is not an entirely new concept. Animism and cinema (especially animation) are closely related in their projection of personhood on animals, plants, objects, and landscapes. The French director Jean Epstein famously wrote that

one of the greatest powers of cinema is its animism. On screen, nature is never inanimate. Objects take on airs. Trees gesticulate. Mountains, just like Etna, convey meanings. Every prop becomes a character. The sets are cut to pieces and each fragment assumes a distinctive expression. An astonishing pantheism is reborn in the world and fills it until it bursts. (Keller & Paul, 2012: 289)

In order to arrive at a shamanic form of cinematic animism, Colectivo Los Ingrávidos embraces a materialist approach to filmmaking. Experimental film techniques such as superimposition, in-camera editing, gestural cinematography, hand developing, and the incorporation of 'end rolls' (flaring when the film runs out) and other aberrations push against the limits of legibility. The best option for the spectator is to let go and let the images and sounds wash over them, and be rewarded with a transcendental experience. True to the collective's futurist ambitions, their shamanic materialism whirls across the centre of power as well as across the fringe, disrespecting the borders that have been drawn in the earth by colonial masters. It is no coincidence that these borders and the subsequent definitions of land use and ownership are at the heart of the postcolonial discussion. Demarcation of the land, ownership, and so-called value creation are colonial strategies that result in the uprooting and disenfranchising of Indigenous people. Imagining the annulment of land ownership is no less than a thought crime in the eyes of the average capitalist. The objective of land ownership is to exploit natural resources by (industrial) farming, mining, or other means, such as leasing the land back to deprived farmers. These practices are manifestly connected to environmental decline and global warming. Personhood, accountability, and freedom are important concepts in the context of climate change. Legal entities such as oil corporations can fight international law, while rivers and mountains cannot defend themselves. A multinaturalist worldview in which other-than-humans are considered persons interferes with this scheme. The Indigenous futurism of Sky Hopinka and Colectivo Los Ingrávidos therefore inspires new ways of thinking ecologically as well.

In popular culture, specifically in mainstream science fiction, nature often takes the back seat. Human culture sits at the top of the pyramid, acting as an overlord in charge of all things natural: earth, stones, rivers, and the animals and plants living therein. In a world heading for climate chaos, Eshwun's 'intimidating global scenarios' (Eshwun, 2003: 292) have now reached a global dimension, albeit still heavily tilted toward the Global South. The now visible effects of climate change and the political impotence to tackle this disaster are reflected in the widespread application of dystopian scenarios in contemporary science fiction films, games, and novels. Imagining a 'naturefuture' is apparently not an easy task. However, this idea lies at the heart of my experimental film project *The Mulch Spider's Dream* (2018).

Enthused by my findings during the making of *Wilderness Series* (see chapter 9), I decided that I wanted to explore plants as signifiers, opening up the possibility that plants have something to 'say', imagining a *future* in which humans and plants communicate. During my stay in Pikin Slee, I had learned to look at plants in a different way. My hosts took me to see the village and the surrounding forest and showed me their way of living and working. They invited me to take part in a ceremonial assembly under a centuries-old mango tree in the centre of the village. The tree *is* the centre of the village – this is the place where the settlement was established. Upon taking me deeper into the forest, the artists paused at what to me first seemed to be a random spot. They pointed out that the appearance of a particular plant on both sides of the path signified that this was the border between the village and the forest. At this location, we were stepping through a portal and we had to change our behaviour accordingly. The rules of the village were now being replaced by rules determined by the forest. Instead of looking for written words or traffic signs, the Saamaka can 'read' their surroundings by looking at naturally occurring phenomena. It took me six years to find out how I could apply this knowledge in my own life and filmmaking practice. Finally, I combined my newly found method, the application of plants as mark makers, with new theoretical insights. Rosi Braidotti proposes a renewed relationship with the earth when she writes 'I am a she-wolf, a breeder that multiplies cells in all directions; I am an incubator and a carrier of vital and lethal viruses; I am mother-earth, the generator of the future' (Braidotti, 2013: 80). This is helpful for a rethinking of concepts like 'innovation', 'progress', and 'science fiction'.

At the time, I was living in a rented house in Cambridge with an English-style garden at the back, which had been only marginally maintained by the previous tenants. Native, perennial plants had come back and were thriving. To me it made a lot of sense to focus on these plants, looking at them as inheritors of the land. Not only does the land serve as the source and breeding ground for plants, but their form, size, and chemical and cellular makeup also provide aesthetic 'input'. Making animations with these tiny and fragile pieces of living material requires a certain attention to the plants' appearance, reactivity, and relative size. Through a process of comparing the repetitive internal structure of the leaves and petals to the film frame and laying out the organic material in appropriate patterns, a fluttering, pulsating, or quivering movement is achieved in projection. This meticulous work took place in a little shed, which allowed me to shield the filmstrips from wind while also providing shade, necessary for slowing down the process on sunny days. Many spiders surrounded me, building their webs in corners and between objects. Tiny spiders crawled out of the gathered organic material, enlivening my workbench in an unexpected way. Each newly animated filmstrip supplied me with additional knowledge: I was learning experientially how plants and film frames could coexist in a meaningful way, spinning my own web alongside my eight-legged companions (see figure 10.3).

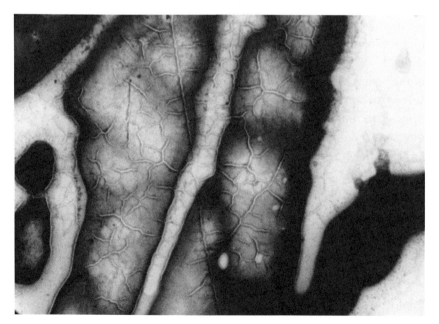

Figure 10.3 *The Mulch Spider's Dream* – Karel Doing (UK 2018, 16mm film, colour, 14min).

The editing process started while the finished strips were drying on a rack. This allowed me to look closely at the resulting patterns, select the best results, and decide on their 'order of appearance'. I took the final roll with me on a journey to Canada, where I was invited to share my ideas at Philip Hoffman's Film Farm (see chapter 8). After an intense week of creating, learning, teaching, and sharing, I was given the opportunity to work at the Liaison of Independent Filmmakers of Toronto (LIFT). I used their Oxberry machine to rephotograph my original footage while altering its speed, changing the exposure, skipping frames, and inserting black frames. Back home, I projected the resulting sequence several times, pondering over possible soundtracks, spiders still occupying the nooks and crannies of my predominantly human habitat. I came across Eleanor Morgan's evocative *Gossamer Days* and learned that spiders 'have relatively poor eyesight and must use their acoustic-vibratory senses to detect and communicate with the world around them' (Morgan, 2016: 111). A spider's frequency range lies between 40 and 600 Hertz, from low hum to the sound of a buzzing insect. When I arrived at the Lumen Crypt Gallery in Bethnal Green to project my still-silent film, peculiar low frequencies surrounded me. The heavy walls reverberated with the muffled sounds of passing traffic, while the space itself produced an eerie reverberation. I collected fallen branches from the adjacent park, brought in two bamboo flutes, and gathered my tools and materials such as tape and various pieces of metal and wood. I used this collection of objects to create sounds while closely listening to the passing trains and buses. The whole space turned into a musical instrument, corresponding to a spider's auditory perception.

The completed film reflects the process of working in close unison with plants and spiders, learning more about a plant's and a spider's awareness through observation, trial and error, iteration, and by doing further literature research. Almost the entire film is bathed in an amber glow induced by the plant chemistry, natural light, and expired film stock. The colours refer to a plant's interiority, rather than confirming the prevalent 'greenness' of plants. Plants absorb light as one of their main sources of energy – their green appearance (for the human eye) is the result of the wavelengths not absorbed and reflected back into the world. Therefore, the amber glow helps us move beyond appearances and delve into the unknown realm of a plant's being in the world. The chemical imprints left by the plants on the film reveal further information about the plants' internal makeup, presenting vascular and cellular assemblages. Some of the images are similar to close-up photography of entangled human bodies: a jumble of arms, legs, and torsos. Other instances are more abstract, as if the shapes were painted on the film with a fine-haired brush or blotted onto the surface with a pipette. Together, these alternations between the microscopic, the corporeal, and the abstract create an other-worldly actuality, a tiny or enormous space without easily recognisable referents. The low frequencies and reverberations on the soundtrack draw these images into a gothic realm, placing the imagery on the inside of an undefined, possibly vast and complex space. In order to provide a short description for the film, I have referred to Thomas Nagel's famous essay 'What Is It Like to Be a Bat?': 'Even without the benefit of philosophical reflection, anyone who has spent some time in an enclosed space with an excited bat knows what it is to encounter a fundamentally alien form of life' (Nagel, 1974: 438). This point of view underscores the redundancy of spaceships for encountering alien life forms. All we need to do is get on our knees or look into small spaces that serve as a refuge for spiders and other tiny creatures to discover an abundance of largely unknown activity. It is in these humble quarters that the concept of naturefuture I was pursuing started to take shape.

The different futurisms that are discussed above – Afrofuturism, Indigenous futurism, and naturefuture – each pursue in their own way a reimagining of past, present, and future in order to rethink historicised accounts of colonialism and racial bias. In all three cases, progress is not a straight line but rather a meandering path that circles back in unexpected ways, providing new vistas of previously embattled or neglected locations and identities. In a reversal of the science fiction genre, technology only plays a relatively minor role, while cultural practices take centre stage. The secret technology mentioned at the start of *The Last Angel of History* is tellingly a cultural artefact – the Blues; in Hopinka's work, oral culture and songs take on a similar role; Colectivo Los Ingrávidos unleash a Meso-American spell by means of shamanic materialism; and in my own work, plants and spiders participate in a process of signification. The future is a process made by the hands of those who dare to be bold.

11

Bloom

Lifestyle choices such as veganism, zero waste, and other environmentally inspired innovations only make a difference when adopted by a large percentage of the populace. The same is true within the arts: a more ecologically aware approach needs to be shared. Taking exclusive ownership of a particular idea or technique might help an individual artist to be successful, but won't have a broader impact. Ecological awareness and behavioural change are based on knowledge, both in a cognitive and in an embodied, tactile form. This can be called a form of literacy: eco-literacy.

Following this line of thought, I decided that I had to find ways to share my discoveries instead of trying to trademark them. I had started using the terms 'phytogram' and 'phytography' to describe the phytochemical traces that I was making. After gaining enough experience with my newly discovered technique, I started looking for opportunities to share my knowledge by giving workshops. The first of a long string of workshops took place in 2018 at LUX, an arts organisation that supports and promotes visual artists working with the moving image (LUX, 2021). This organisation had recently relocated their offices to Waterlow Park in Highgate, London. The park is home to a wide variety of trees, bushes, grasses, herbs, and flowers, which makes it an exceptionally good location for a practice that involves plants in image making. I started the workshop with an introduction about my findings, immediately followed by a hands-on demonstration with expired paper and film as basic materials in a bid to minimise the environmental footprint of the event. The participants gathered leaves and petals in the park, and, after doing some initial experiments on photographic paper, the group created direct animations on 16mm filmstrips that ran across the outdoor tables (see figure 11.1). After plenty of sunlight

Figure 11.1 Phytography workshop, Aberystwyth University (UK 2022); photograph by Trish Kiy.

exposure, the organic material was removed from the filmstrips, and the images were fixed. While the newly made animations were drying, several experimental films from the organisation's archive and distribution collection were screened in the exhibition space. The film programme was curated around the themes of the workshop – ecology, plants, landscape, and direct animation – and included work by filmmakers such as Stan Brakhage, Rose Lowder, Kayla Parker, and Vicky Smith. Finally, the phytograms were spliced together in loops and projected with two projectors (side by side). The participants responded enthusiastically, and a fruitful discussion about art and ecology marked a first successful attempt at knowledge exchange. The workshop results prompted me to collect further plant material from the park, to take advantage of the variety of different species to hand. The next day, I rolled out a long strip of film on the path running through the middle of my backyard in Cambridge, using the leaves and seed pods that I had gathered in Waterlow Park, building on the outcome of the workshop in an experiential way. This made me realise that the workshop had not only provided me with an opportunity to share my ideas but also had enriched my own practice in a way that I had not expected. Additionally, I made a dedicated website titled *Phytogram – Plants, Chemistry, Photography, Film* (Doing, 2018) and recorded a set of video tutorials. During the COVID-19 pandemic, visitor numbers grew exponentially and requests for online workshops started coming in – from London, Seattle, Boston, Vancouver, Detroit, Mexico City, Washington, Rio de Janeiro, Tromsø, and Halifax. More and more experimental film-makers started using phytography in their work, for example Caryn Cline, Benjamin Wigley, Bruno Varela, Federica Foglia, Emma Piper-Burket, and Kathryn Ramey. Photographers such as Milena Michalski, Wiebke Rost, Anne Eder, Sophie Sherwood, and Karen Hymer also started integrating phytography into their work. Blog posts and online videos started appearing alongside articles in magazines and journals. Universities, museums, and art centres started including phytogram workshops in their programmes. After receiving numerous workshop pictures, digital reproductions, links to online videos, and emails from fellow filmmakers and photographers, I decided to compile an artist book with a selection of these images and words. The project was financed through crowdfunding and sold out in a few months. My strategy had worked: the technique had acquired a life of its own.

During the workshops that I led in person, the process of collective knowledge building continued. As already mentioned in chapter 10, Philip Hoffman had invited me to participate as an artist in residence in Film Farm 2018. He introduced me to sound recording film, a cheaply available 16mm film stock. This type of film is optimised for creating optical soundtracks and therefore the emulsion has a characteristic quality, fine grain, and high contrast. The weather in Ontario was exceptionally hot, and the light was very bright. It turned out that these conditions generated bright pink, purple, and yellow colour effects on the otherwise transparent parts of the filmstrip. I experimented with a combination of camera images and phytography, spurred on by the reversal baths that were made available in the darkrooms. I shot a series of portraits of my fellow participants, processed the film until the re-exposure step, took the processed and bleached film out of the darkroom and covered the remaining emulsion with local plants such as milkweed, wild peas, and long blades of grass. This process results in a superimposition of camera image and phytographic image, with a shifting emphasis on either lens- or plant-based image depending on the subtly veering balance between both inscriptions. The next year, I received an invitation for a short residency from Analogue Farm, an initiative based in Lancashire that takes inspiration from its Canadian counterpart. The weather there was cold and windy. Local plant species include ferns, hawthorn bushes, and many varieties of blooming grasses. In this environment, the colour effects leaned toward dark shades of green, earthy reds, and yellows. The more austere landscape and flora prompted me to create repetitive compositions on the filmstrip, aiming for a specificity of animated movement rather than a feast of different shapes and rhythms. After each workshop, residency, and home experiment, my reel of phytogram animations grew further. After two years of teaching, learning, and collecting, I reviewed the reel and selected a number of 'scenes' for an eight-minute-long film simply titled *Phytography* (2020). With the collected footage approached as a found object, the creativity and expressive qualities of the plants themselves are brought forward, thus inviting the spectator to discover the subtle differences in tone, texture, form, and rhythm. The film starts with a series of short sequences based on patterns that are created on the filmstrip, with the goal being regularity and congruence. This rigidity is abandoned little by little further into the film, building toward a dense flow of forms, rhythms, and colours. The majority of the film is made on sound recording film, a material that, under favourable circumstances, produces a variety of pink and purple tones when exposed to the ultraviolet rays of the sun. Further nuances in colour are influenced by plant chemistry, the translucency of the leaves and petals, and the availability of sunlight. Also, some footage is made on long-expired camera negative, rendering more sombre dark brown and grey tones. Distinct forms such as starred seed pods and zigzagged leaf edges stand out of the chaos. These direct animations are interspersed with short sequences made on photographic paper, which allows more precise arrangements. Finally, the film moves toward complete abstraction with a sequence in which streaks of chemistry fly in all directions. The process of making this film was generative: teaching and learning were entwined.

Teaching is prevalently understood as a purely human affair. We can train a dog and teach our pet to fetch a stick, but from an anthropocentric perspective, there is nothing to be learned from the animal. We can breed a plant and, through a process of selection, improve our yield. Again, a reversal of roles would be met with ridicule. These presumptions are poetically overturned by Robin Wall Kimmerer, a mother, scientist, decorated professor, and enrolled member of the Citizen Potawatomi Nation. In her book *Braiding Sweetgrass*, she writes about the teachings of plants:

We say that humans have the least experience with how to live and thus the most to learn – we must look to our teachers among the other species for guidance. Their wisdom is apparent in the way that they live. They teach us by example. They've been on the earth far longer than we have been, and have had time to figure things out. They live both above and below ground, joining Skyworld to the earth. Plants know how to make food and medicine from light and water, and then they give it away. (Kimmerer, 2013: 21-22)

In the following chapters, Kimmerer carefully underpins her thesis with multiple examples, some personal, others professional, bridging the gap between her personal life and her career as a scientist. Her point of view is valuable in the context of my own practice, particularly my experiments with phytography. Instead of manipulating the plant in order to make it produce the desired image, another approach could be to 'follow the plant'. When making phytograms on motion picture film, the imprints that the plants leave on the filmstrip are animated during projection. This can be fairly chaotic, with blobs and splashes dashing alongside more recognisable formations and patterns. But cinema phytography can be taken a step further: the repetitive elements that can be found in plants suggest a coincidence with the division of a filmstrip into frames. When this coincidence is teased out, the animated image starts to move in a more specific way, producing pulsating, gyrating, quivering, or scintillating effects. There is nothing new here: these are the principles of direct animation that can be achieved in multiple ways, such as painting, drawing, and stencilling on film. This approach is well known and goes as far back as Len Lye's *A Colour Box* (1935), and Norman McLaren's and Evelyn Lambart's *Begone Dull Care* (1949). Besides these historicised examples, contemporary experimental filmmakers have used their own bodily residue to make moving images. Notable examples are Thorsten Fleisch's *Blutrausch* (1999), Emma Hart's *Skin Film 2* (2005-2007), and Vicky Smith's *Noisy Licking, Dribbling and Spitting* (2014). Fleisch creates images with his own blood directly on the film's emulsion. The spectator is confronted with lumps, clots, and clumps of coagulated blood cells dancing across the screen. The filmmaker provides a further context with the following statement: 'I was interested in literally getting *inside* the mechanics of film projection, and took something that is most vital to me, my blood, for a tour through the insides of a projector and then viewed the result on the screen' (Fleisch 2009: 193). Similarly, Hart peeled off the top layer of her own skin with cellotape and transposed the affixed cells to clear leader, thus creating a literal coincidence between her own skin and the 'skin' of film. In the third example, *Noisy Licking, Dribbling and Spitting*, Smith chews berries and uses the coloured spit to mark the emulsion, producing an experience that is both intimate and provocative. Writing about these films, Kim Knowles observes that

the viewer is positioning in some 'sense' within the body of the filmmaker, and, crucially, the body of the film. The marks made on the film thus not only testify to the hand of the artist, the trace of a physical connection with the material, but also, more profoundly, they represent a fusion of two organic bodies. (Knowles, 2013)

Phytogram animations contribute to this inquiry by extending the senses beyond the human body, incorporating plant bodies in a similar fusion. It is not only the artist but also the plant who partakes in the making of the film, through physical contact between plant and photographic emulsion. To make this work, the filmmaker needs to observe the quality of the plant in great detail. Size, internal structure, flexibility, transparency, and chemical makeup all matter. In turn, this requires a further study of plant growth and an awareness of the seasons, the local weather, and the distribution of species in a garden or landscape. This helps to build a relationship with plants that goes beyond exploitation, a relationship that is shaped by an exchange of information between plant, human, and image. The marks left by the plants transmogrify into inscriptions and a more complete form of 'plant writing' is achieved. What grows here is a specific form of shared knowledge that relates to earth, rain, rhythm, movement, chemistry, and light – a form of knowledge that might be knowable by both humans and plants.

Human language is not a realm that can be shared constructively with non-humans. Social critic and linguist Noam Chomsky has articulated this convincingly in his article 'Human Language and Other Semiotic Systems' (Chomsky, 1979). Still, there are other ways of communication that might be used to bridge the gap between us and other species. The title of Chomsky's article implies a way forward: in order to communicate across species, it could be useful to look at *other semiotic systems*. This is exactly what is done by biosemioticians. The foundational thesis of biosemiotics – an area of research that has been growing in recent decades – was formulated in a profoundly concise way by Thomas Sebeok, an American semiotician seen as one of the most prominent scholars within the field: 'Life and semiosis are coextensive' (Kull, Emmeche & Favareau, 2011: 69). This thesis leads to a view of biology beyond the physiological or the material, a biology based on the exchange of *information* in living systems. Such an inquiry can be described as qualitative rather than quantitative, and as such it implies a possible shift in biological research. The Cartesian view of plants or animals is that their responses can be explained as being 'hardwired'. As they take cues from their environment, sensations are translated into 'automatic' behavioural traits. This explanation removes the need for cognition beyond the human. This line of thought is reinforced by behaviourism, a theory made popular by the American psychologist B.F. Skinner and his famous experiments with pigeons and rats that used a system of rewards and punishments to control their actions (see further Skinner, 2009). Animal behaviour is seen as being based on conditioned responses, lacking any form of intelligence. However, in contemporary ethology (the science of animal behaviour), building on the groundbreaking research of the Nobel Prize–winning biologist Nikolaas Tinbergen, animal behaviour is seen as much more complex, influenced by a set of different stimuli and responses that include anticipation, learning, and memory. This shared form of cognition beyond the human is central to biosemiotic research as well:

> If biosemiotics has any one single most constructive message to give the mainstream scientific community, surely it is precisely this: a semiotic process is not a ghostly, mental, human thought process. Rather, it is, in the first instance, nothing more nor less mysterious than that natural interface by which an organism actively negotiates the present demands of its internal biological organization with the present demands of the organization of its external surround. (Favareau, 2010: 32)

Notably, in this carefully worded statement, the writer uses the word 'organism', including not only animals but also plants and microorganisms in semiotic processes. Analogous to their relationship with animals, humans have domesticated plants for thousands of years, for example, species like rice and maize. The story behind the domestication of rice is complex and fascinating. Multidisciplinary research shows that there was not a single domestication event but several (see further Sweeney & McCouch, 2007). The best-known event occurred in the lower Yangzi River valley in China, but a second event took place in the Niger Delta in Africa, and there was likely a third one on the Australian continent. This final occurrence is only mentioned as an aside in the literature, but it is convincingly supported by citizen science, documented in detail by Bruce Pascoe in his book *Dark Emu* (Pascoe, 2014). The different varieties of rice have different characteristics, demonstrating the ability of the plant to adapt to a variety of climatic and cultural circumstances. Another important food staple, maize, has been domesticated only once, an event that can be traced to the Balsas River valley in Meso-America. Unravelling its genetic history has been particularly difficult as maize's wild ancestor has been notoriously difficult to trace (see further Tian, Stevens & Buckler, 2009). Both examples demonstrate a close cultural relationship between humans and plants that has received little attention in academic research. A scientific approach such as biosemiotics can help to unravel some of the qualitative aspects of this relationship.

A comparable point of view on the omnipresence of semiotic processes appears in contemporary anthropology. In his book *How Forests Think*, anthropologist Eduardo Kohn investigates how the Runa Indians in Ecuador navigate the rainforest aided by close observations of the behaviour of animals and their natural surroundings. By showing that certain sounds are significant for both animals and humans, the writer demonstrates how meaning can move in and out of the human domain. According to Kohn, signs cannot be precisely located in sounds, events, words, bodies, or minds 'because they are ongoing relational processes; (Kohn, 2015: 33). The Runa are highly skilled in understanding these relational processes, as exemplified by their skill in catching flying ants who emerge from their nests only once a year within a short timeframe.

The ants will fly out only when circumstances are optimal, influenced by a range of factors such as fruiting regimes, meteorological conditions, and the habitual behaviour of predators like bats and birds. Bats hunt at night and will cease their activity in the early morning, while birds take over shortly after sunrise. The ants benefit from the short time slot in between. Kohn concludes that 'people attempt to enter some of the logic of the semiotic network that structures ant life' (ibid., 80). The Brazilian anthropologist Eduardo Viveiros de Castro (mentioned in chapter 10) takes up the subject in his book *Cannibal Metaphysics* (Viveiros de Castro, 2017). He approaches the idea of a shared human/animal realm in broader terms, investigating Amerindian shamanism. Instead of a comparative study, Viveiros de Castro attempts to uncover the philosophical building blocks through a perspectivist methodology. He coins the term 'multi-naturalism' in an analogy to the Western idea of multiculturalism. Instead of looking at others from a standpoint assuming differences in culture, Amerindian shamanism looks at others from a standpoint of difference in 'nature'. Subsequently, perspectives between humans and animals can be swapped:

In seeing us as nonhumans, animals and spirits regard themselves (their own species) as human: they perceive their food – jaguars see blood as manioc beer, vultures see the worms in rotten meat as grilled fish – their corporeal attributes (coats, feathers, claws, beaks) as finery or cultural instruments, and they organize their social systems in the same way as human institutions, with chiefs, shamans, exogamous moieties and rituals. (Ibid., 57)

Transposing this concept to plants is challenging as plants do not have mouths, eyes, or hands/claws. However, plants certainly do take in nutrition, respond to light, and are able to navigate specific spatial circumstances above- and underground. Moreover, the research of Suzanne W. Simard has revolutionised our understanding of plants as communicators (see further: Simard et al., 1997). Simard and her colleagues used a technique called 'reciprocal isotope labelling' to track the exchange of nutrients between trees. The experiment showed that trees and mycorrhizal fungi behave in a mutualist way by forming an underground network that not only enables the exchange of nutrients but also the exchange of signals between different species. These interconnections have been termed the 'wood wide web' in both the scientific community and among artists and environmentalists:

The whole system is integrated, holistic and complex, and a new area of research has emerged which aims to understand inter-plant communication at the molecular level. It appears that plants may use a form of 'language', in which different molecules act as 'words', although the precise nature of the dialogue has yet to be deciphered. (Rhodes, 2017: 335)

Encouraged by Kimmerer's concept of 'plants as teachers', Sebeok's 'biosemiotics', Viveiros de Castro's 'multinaturalism', and Simard's 'wood wide web', I was able to refine my phytography animations while working on my film *A Perfect Storm* (2022). I worked on 35mm film, taking advantage of the much larger size of each film frame. I made a series of animated strips with the tiny elements of inflorescences, seeds harvested from grasses and sorrel, and shredded stems. These particles were scattered on the film, and I relied on the inherent self-organisation of each distinct form. As a counterpart, I created additional sequences that were heavily composed, working with comparatively larger petals and leaves, creating repetitive patterns on the filmstrip. To make these, I gathered native plants such as clover, hawkbit, herb robert, and goldenrod. I experimented with different forms of organisation, recreating the ecosystem that I found in my garden on the filmstrip, joining a variety of forms together. Additionally, I used the particular form and appearance of single species, focusing more on the regularity of a particular leaf or flower (see figure 11.2). In all cases, I took cues from the plants, either in a sort of laissez-faire style by scattering particles, by observing the plants in their own habitat, or by letting the shape of the plant determine how the different elements fitted together. The filmstrips were presoaked with the solution of vitamin C and soda in order to create a dark background and achieve maximal detail. Some plants, such as the goldenrod, have cells that are big enough to be seen in projection. Other very fine details of the plant, such as the vascular system, also become visible with this improved way of making phytograms. After patterns and sequences were composed on the filmstrip, the raw footage was edited, taking the local windy and wet weather and the Oxfordshire landscape as cues. I combined field recordings with an improvised guitar track and used a variety

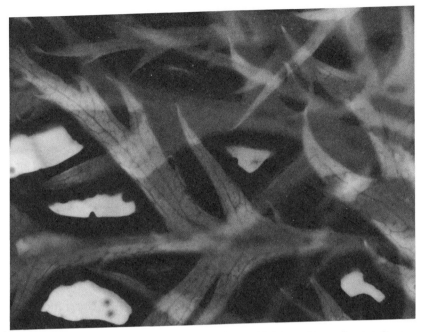

Figure 11.2 *A Perfect Storm* – Karel Doing (UK 2022, 16mm film, colour and bw, 3min).

of different projection speeds to create a series of miniature vistas. As a surprise element, I added an animated sequence of gargoyles. In Oxford, many old and new university buildings feature grotesque human, animal, and hybrid heads. These carvings can be described as humorous or fantastic but also provide a connection with a worldview in which animals, plants, and humans are intertwined. Such a 'primitive' element struck my attention in a city that is very focused on determinism and reductionism.

Phytography is a practice that can reveal plants as creative beings. Instead of viewing plants and animals as inert, merely following entirely predictable schemes, I consider the entire biosphere to be a place brimming with meaning and expression. This is a risky concept in a world that is dominated by anthropocentrism:

Being objects, not subjects, one does not enter into contact with plants or animals. And should anyone do so – perceive and treat nonhumans as persons on an equal standing with oneself qua human – it would not be regarded as an innocent mistake, a neutral error, for which one may be easily excused. (Vetlesen, 2019: 157)

In line with a perspective that considers plants as creative entities, the term 'phytography' suggests that some kind of 'writing' is taking place. This touches on another contested terrain: language as a purely human domain or language as a realm that can exist beyond the human. As David Abram argues:

The earthly terrain in which we find ourselves, and upon which we depend for all nourishment, is shot through with suggestive scrawls and traces, from the sinuous calligraphy of rivers winding across the land, inscribing arroyos and canyons into the parched earth of the desert, to the black slash burned by lightning into the trunk of an old elm. (Abram, 2017: 95)

In phytography, plants do leave such 'scrawls and traces' on the surface of the photochemical medium. Initially these can be quite chaotic, but with careful observation and gentle forms of persuasion, the difficult-to-decipher randomness grows into a meaningful pattern. Plants become partners in the creative process, inscribing meaningful traces on photochemical film. Beyond the engagement of the spectator in the construction of meaning, which was one of the aims of the structural/materialist filmmakers of the '70s, in phytography the subject (the plant) is also engaged in a process of making meaning. Language, then, buds (literally as well as figuratively) from nature and accumulates, step by step, into a format that is legible within the human realm.

My most recent phytography-based film *Oxygen* (2023) is made entirely with blades of grass. Each blade stretches out over multiple frames, widening and narrowing again within a timeframe of one to two seconds. It is a common expression that no straight lines exist in nature, but a minute-long observation of a blade of grass contradicts this presumption. The phytographic images of the blades demonstrate this surprising regularity with multiple lines running in parallel (see figure 11.3). The lines are offset by small dots   concentrations of phytochemistry – occurring in a much more chaotic pattern, scattered randomly across the innards of the grass. The total effect is one of speed. The blades run across the screen as if travelling down a strange highway exceeding the speed

Figure 11.3 *Oxygen* – Karel Doing (UK 2023, 16mm film, colour, 6min).

limit, sparks flying off in all directions. The film is as simple as it is confusing, putting the grass in an entirely different perspective, as opposed to the ultimate anthropocentric symbolism of a manicured golf course. Grass unleashed.

Afterword

This book ends in a fleeting moment called the present. Of course there will be a delay between me writing this down and you reading these words. Another chapter could be added now, and a new book will be written soon. Experimental film practice is very much alive. At the moment of writing, the four-year project SPECTRAL is ongoing, a collaboration between six European artist-run film labs. On the other side of the Atlantic, the Liaison of Independent Filmmakers Toronto (LIFT) is hosting a gathering on the theme of resilience. Change is constant, everything is in process. Simultaneously, the future of film – especially photochemical film – is uncertain, but this does not stop artists from dedicating themselves fully to this unique medium.

In this book, I have attempted to contextualise experimental film in global events and intellectual and political movements. Instead of being an artform from the past, experimental film is responsive to these currents and in some cases can even be seen as a harbinger, ahead of its time. It has taken me many years to dissect my own thoughts and ideas as an insider and enthusiastic practitioner who uses a generative, improvisational, and holistic approach. My book and my films are answerable to Ursula K. Le Guin's carrier bag theory: 'Put something you want, because it's useful, edible or beautiful, into a bag, or a basket, or a bit of rolled bark or leaf, or a net woven of your own hair, or what have you, and then take it home with you, a home being another, larger kind of pouch or bag, a container for people' (Le Guin, 2018: 166).

What this book reveals is a practice of wandering, searching, and researching. An embrace of variance, a favouring of the question mark. There is no chance of complete control or predictability. The better option is to treat surprises with glee, bending like a tree during a powerful storm, changing colour like a white butterfly in a coal mine, or feeding on radiation in the sarcophagus of an exploded nuclear reactor. The films that I have discussed in this book do not achieve such incredible feats. What drives me to make such a comparison is the contradictory presence of imagination and truth – in other words, the coincidence of abstraction and realism in contemporary experimental filmmaking. Who needs a linear narrative in the company of such a rich enigma?

Bibliography

Abram, David (1997) *The Spell of the Sensuous: Perception and Language in a More-Than-Human World*, New York: Vintage Books.

Agawu, Kofi (1995) 'The Invention of "African Rhythm"', *Journal of the American Musicological Society* 48, no. 3, Music Anthropologies and Music Histories (Autumn 1995): 380–395.

Ameur, Zoubida, Hamidouche, Wassim, François, Edouard, Radosavljević, Miloš, Menard, Daniel & Demarty, Claire-Hélène (2022) 'Deep-Based Film Grain Removal and Synthesis', *arXiv preprint arXiv:2206.07411*, https://arxiv.org/abs/2206.07411 (accessed 12 January 2023).

Bailey, Derek (1980) *Improvisation: Its Nature and Practice in Music*, Boston: Da Capo Press.

Barad, Karen (2007) *Meeting the Universe Halfway: Quantum Physics and the Entanglement of Matter and Meaning*, Durham, NC: Duke University Press.

Bell, Janis, C. (2008) 'Sfumato and Acuity Perspective', in Farago, Claire (ed.), *Leonardo Da Vinci and the Ethics of Style,* Manchester: Manchester University Press, 161–188.

Benjamin, Walter (2007) *Illuminations*, New York: Schocken Books.

Bennett, Jane (2010) *Vibrant Matter: A Political Ecology of Things*, Durham, NC: Duke University Press.

Bering-Porter, David (2014) 'The Automaton in All of Us: Gifs, Cinemagraphs and the Films of Martin Arnold', *Moving Image Review & Art Journal (Miraj)* 3, no. 2: 178–192.

Bey, Hakim (1985) *T.A.Z.: The Temporary Autonomous Zone, Ontological Anarchy, Poetic Terrorism*, New Haven, CT: Anarchist Library.

Bliss, Lauren (2016) 'On Lab Laba Laba (Spider Lab) and the Playful Reincarnation of the Propaganda Films of New Order Era Indonesia', *Desistfilm,* https://desistfilm.com/on-lab-laba-laba-spider-lab-and-the-playful-reincarnation-of-the-propaganda-films-of-new-order-era-indonesia/ (accessed 14 December 2022).

Boggs, Carl (1977) 'Revolutionary Process, Political Strategy, and the Dilemma of Power', *Theory and Society* 4, no. 3: 359–393.

Braidotti, Rosi (2013) *The Posthuman*, London: Polity Press.

Broomer, Stephen (2023) *Revelations by Sunlight Translation, Monument and Metaphor in Colectivo los Ingrávidos's The Sun Quartet*, Toronto: AD HOC.

Brynntrup, Michael (1959–∞) *Biographie,* http://www.brynntrup.de/ (accessed 9 August 2022).

Castro, Vinícus Portella (2022) 'Noise and Signal as Ground and Figure: Emergence and Interference in Media Ecologies', *Humanities and Social Sciences Communications* 9, no. 209.

Catanese, Rossella & Parikka, Jussi (2018) 'Handmade Films and Artist-Run Labs: The Chemical Sites of Film's Counterculture', *Necsus*, November 23, 1918, https://necsus-ejms. org/handmade-films-and-artist-run-labs-the-chemical-sites-of-films-counterculture/ (accessed 24 May 2023).

Chapman, Andrew (2011) 'Pavel Kostomarov and Aleksandr Rastorguev: "I Love You (Ya tebia liubliu, 2011)"', *Kinokultura* 34: http://www.kinokultura.com/2011/34r-liubliutebia.shtml (accessed 26 April 2019).

Chodorov, Pip (2014) 'The Artist-Run Film Labs', *Millennium Film Journal* N60 (Fall 2014): 28–36.

Chomsky, Noam (1979) 'Human Language and Other Semiotic Systems', *Semiotica* 25, no. 1–2: 43.

Colectivo Los Ingrávidos (2022) 'Shamanic Materialism: 77 Thesis on the Audiovisual', in Della Noce, Elio & Murari, Lucas (eds.), *Expanded Nature: Écologies du Cinéma Expérimental*, Paris: Lightcone, 187–194.

Cox, Christoph (2011) 'Beyond Representation and Signification: Toward a Sonic Materialism', *Journal of Visual Culture* 10, no. 2: 145–161.

Darwin, Charles (1981) *The Descent of Men and Selection in Relation to Sex*, Princeton, NJ: Princeton University Press.

Davis, Duane (1995) 'Lydia Lunch: Punishment of the Rose', in Sargeant, Jack (ed.), *Deathtripping: The Cinema of Transgression*, London: Creation Books, 177–184.

Doing, Karel (2017) 'Ambient Poetics and Critical Posthumanism in Expanded Cinema', PhD thesis, University of the Arts London, https://ualresearchonline.arts.ac.uk/id/eprint/12393/ (accessed 9 September 2022).

Doing, Karel (2018) *Phytogram – Plants, Chemistry, Photography, Film*, https://phytogram. blog/ (accessed 20 April 2023).

Doing, Karel (2020) 'Phytograms: Rebuilding Human-Plant Affiliations', *Animation* 15, no. 1: 22–36.

Doing, Karel (2022) 'Les Réalités Désordonnées du Cinéma Multispécifique', in Della Noce, Elio & Murari, Lucas (eds.), *Expanded Nature: Écologies du Cinéma Expérimental*, Paris: Lightcone Editions, 87–95.

Doing, Karel (2023) 'Cinema and the Prefigurative', *Culture Unbound* 15, no. 2.

Doing, Karel (2024) 'Experimental Film Practice and the Biosphere', in Knowles, Kim & Walley, Jonathan (eds.), *The Palgrave Handbook of Experimental Film*, London: Palgrave Macmillan.

Dyson, E., Gilder, G., Keyworth, G. & Toffler, A. (1994) 'Cyberspace and the American Dream: A Magna Carta for the Knowledge Age', http://www.pff.org/issues-pubs/ futureinsights/fi1.2magnacarta.html (accessed 20 September 2023).

Echo Park Film Center (2019): *The Sound We See – a Global Slow Film Movement*, http://www.echoparkfilmcenter.org/blog/sound-we-see/ (accessed 30 July 2021).

Eley, Geoff & Nield, Keith (2000) 'Farewell to the Working Class?', *International Labor and Working Class History*, no. 57 (Spring): 1–30.

Elsaesser, Thomas (2019) 'Sigmar Polke: Films', *Framework* 60, no. 1 (Spring): 53–63.

EMAF (2021) *Experimental Film Workshop*, https://www.emaf.de/historie/ (accessed 9 September 2022).

Enns, Clint (2015) 'The Reality-Eater or the Eye-Mouth: An Interview with OJOBOCA (Anja Dornieden and Juan David González Monroy)', *INCITE,* issue #∞ Forever, https://incite-online.net/ojoboca.html (accessed 14 December 2022).

Erzen, Jale (2008) 'The Dervishes Dance – the Sacred Ritual of Love', *Contemporary Aesthetics* 6, article 7, https://digitalcommons.risd.edu/liberalarts_contempaesthetics/vol6/iss1/7 (accessed 20 September 2023).

Eshwun, Kodwo (2003) 'Further Considerations on Afrofuturism', *Cr: The New Centennial Review* 3, no. 2: 287–302.

Extrapool (n.d.) *About KNUST*, https://extrapool.nl/about-knust-press/ (accessed 24 May 2023).

Favereau, Donald (2010) 'Introduction: An Evolutionary History of Biosemiotics', in Favereau, D. (ed.), *Essential Readings in Biosemiotics*, Dordrecht: Springer, 1–77.

Feldman, Seth (2007): 'Vertov after Manovich', *Canadian Journal of Film Studies* 16, no. 1 (Spring): 39–50.

Filmlabs (2022) *Fanzines*, https://www.filmlabs.org/dissemination/fanzines/ (accessed 24 May 2023).

Fisher, Mark (2016) *The Weird and the Eerie*, London: Repeater Books.

Fleisch, Thorsten (2009) 'Borderline Animation', *Animation* 4, no. 2: 191–202.

Forsberg, Walter (2021) 'Underground Impulses: Elena Pardo's Mexican Multimodal Media Praxis', *Post Script: Interviews with Latin American Women Filmmakers* 40, no. 2/3 (Winter–Summer): 94–104, 146–147.

Forster, Tim (2022) 'Contesting Class, Gender and National Identity: The Visual Art Practice of Test Dept', *Punk & Post-Punk* 11, no. 2: 229–250.

Fox, Jason (2018) ' "Where Are Those Lines?": Discussions About and Around Experimental Ethnography with Sky Hopinka, Naeem Mohaiemen and Deborah Stratman', in Windhausen, Federico (ed.), *A Companion to Experimental Cinema*, Hoboken, NJ: Wiley-Blackwell.

Frye, Brian (2003) 'Avant-Garde Film Diary', *Millennium Film Journal* 41, no. 39/40 (Winter): 100–109.

Gamble, Christopher N., Hanan, Joshua S. & Nail, Thomas (2019) 'What Is New Materialism?', *Angelaki* 24, no. 6: 111–134.

Gidal, Peter (1989) *Materialist Film*, Abingdon: Routledge.

Gombrich, Ernst H. (1995) *Art and Illusion: A Study in the Psychology of Pictorial Representation*, London: Phaidon.

Gordon, Uri (2017) 'Prefigurative Politics between Ethical Practice and Absent Promise', *Political Studies* 66, no. 2: 521–537.

Gough, Maria (1999) 'Faktura: The Making of the Russian Avant-Garde', *Res: Anthropology and Aesthetics* 36: 32–59.

Green-Cole, Ruth (2020) 'Painting Blood: Visualizing Menstrual Blood in Art', in Bobel, Chris et al. (eds.), *The Palgrave Handbook of Critical Menstruation Studies*, Singapore: Palgrave Macmillan, 787–801.

Gregory, R. L. (1997) *Eye and Brain: The Psychology of Seeing*, 5th ed., Princeton, NJ: Princeton University Press.

Gunning, Tom (2004) 'Flickers: On Cinema's Power for Evil', in Pomerance, Murray (ed.), *Bad: Infamy, Darkness, Evil and Slime on the Screen*, Albany: SUNY Press.

Gunning, Tom (2009) 'Films that Tell Time', *Moving Image Source*, February 6, http://www.movingimagesource.us/articles/films-that-tell-time-20090206 (accessed 15 September 2022).

Habib, André (2006) 'Ruin Archive and the Time of Cinema: Peter Delpeut's Lyrical Nitrate', *Substance*, 120–139.

Haraway, Donna (1991) 'A Cyborg Manifesto', in *Symians, Cyborgs and Women: The Reinvention of Nature*, New York: Routledge, 149–182.

Haraway, Donna J. (2016) 'Tentacular Thinking: Anthropocene, Capitalocene, Chthulucene', in *Staying with the Trouble: Making Kin in the Chthulucene*. Durham, NC: Duke University Press, 30–57.

Hayles N. Katherine (1999) *How We Became Posthuman: Virtual Bodies in Cybernetics Literature and Informatics*, Chicago: University of Chicago Press.

Haynes, Wiiliams (1952) 'Out of Alchemy into Chemistry', *Scientific Monthly* 75, no. 5 (November): 268–272.

Hegarty, Paul (2009) 'Noise Threshold: Merzbow and the End of Natural Sound', *Organised Sound* 6: 193–200.

Heisenberg, Werner (2000) *Physics and Philosophy*, London: Penguin.

Heynen, Hilde (1996) 'New Babylon: The Antinomies of Utopia', *Assemblage*, no. 29 (April): 24–39.

Hobhouse, Hermione (ed.) (1994) *Survey of London: Volumes 43 and 44, Poplar, Blackwall and Isle of Dogs*, http://www.british-history.ac.uk/survey-london/vols43-4 (accessed 15 September 2022).

Hoffman, Philip (2020) 'Completed Films (1994–2019)', https://philiphoffman.ca/film-farm/completed-films-1994-2010/ (accessed 13 March 2020).

Hogan, Linda (2007) *Dwellings: A Spiritual History of the Living World*, New York: Norton.

Holloway, John (2019) *Change the World without Taking Power,* 4th ed., London: Pluto Press.

Holme, Adrian (2014) 'Alchemy, Image and Text: The Waning of Alchemy and the Decline of Visual Discourse in the Late Renaissance', *Journal of Illustration* 1, no. 2 (October): 189–209.

Huizinga, Johan (2016) *Homo Ludens – A Study of the Play-Element in Culture,* Kettering: Angelico Press.

Hunter, A. (1990) *Theatre of Cinema Takes Shape at Third Eye,* Glasgow: National Review of Live Art.

Institute of International Studies at the University of California, Berkeley (2008) *Film and the Creation of Mind,* https://conversations.berkeley.edu/jacobs_1999 (accessed 15 September 2022).

John, Henry (2015) 'UK Rave Culture and the Thatcherite Hegemony, 1988–94' *Cultural History* 4, no. 2: 162–186.

Jordan, John (1998) 'The Art of Necessity: The Subversive Imagination of Anti-Road Protest and Reclaim the Streets', in McKay, George (ed.), *DiY Culture: Party and Protest in Nineties Britain*, London: Verso, 129–151.

Keller, Sarah & Paul, Jason N. (2012) *Jean Epstein: Critical Essays and New Translations,* Amsterdam: Amsterdam University Press.

Kimmerer, Robin Wall (2013) *Braiding Sweetgrass*, Minneapolis: Milkweed Editions.

Klein, Cecelia F. (1976) 'The Identity of the Central Deity on the Aztec Calendar Stone', *Art Bulletin* 58: 1–12.

Knowles, Kim (2013) 'Blood, Sweat, and Tears: Bodily Inscriptions in Contemporary Experimental Film', *NECSUS: European Journal of Media Studies* 2: 447–463, necsus-ejms.org/blood-sweat-and-tears-bodily-inscriptions-in-contemporary-experimental-film (accessed 26 February 2019).

Knowles, Kim (2020) *Experimental Film and Photochemical Practices*, Cham: Palgrave Macmillan.

Kohl Bines, Rosana (2015) 'Childhood Ghosts with Boltanski and Benjamin', in MacLean, Malcolm, Russell, Wendy & Ryall, Emily (eds.), *Play, Philosophy and Performance,* Abingdon: Routledge, 132–141.

Kohn, Eduardo (2015) *How Forests Think: Toward an Anthropology beyond the Human,* Berkeley: University of California Press.

Krauss, Rosalind (1993) *The Optical Unconscious*, Cambridge, MA: MIT Press.

Krivý, Maroš (2010) 'Industrial Architecture and Negativity: The Aesthetics of Architecture in the Works of Gordon Matta-Clark, Robert Smithson and Bernd and Hilla Becher', *Journal of Architecture* 15, no. 6: 827–852.

Kull, Kalevi, Emmeche, Claus & Favareau, Donald (2011) 'Biosemiotic Research Questions', in Claus, Emmeche & Kull, Kalevi (eds.), *Towards a Semiotic Biology*, London: Imperial College Press, 67–90.

Kuzniar, Alice, A. (2022) 'The Queer German Cinema: Michael Brynntrup', in Brynntrup, Michael (ed.), *Super 8*, Berlin: Salzgeber Buchverlage GmbH, 380–385.

l'Abominable (2022) 'Catalogue', https://www.l-abominable.org/en/catalog/ (accessed 14 December 2022).

Lee, Pamela M. (2000) *Object to Be Destroyed – the Work of Gordon Matta-Clarke*, Cambridge, MA: MIT Press.

Le Guin, Ursula K. (2018) *Dreams Must Explain Themselves: The Selected Non-Fiction of Ursula K. Le Guin*, London: Gollancz.

Leite, Ricardo (2022) *Biodegradable Film Processing*, https://ricardoleite.org/2022/10/05/biodegradable-film-processing/ (accessed 13 January 2023).

Lenoir, Tim (2002) 'Makeover: Writing the Body into the Posthuman Technoscape. Part One: Embracing the Posthuman', *Configurations* 10, no. 2: 203–220.

Lippard, Chris & Johnson, Guy (1993) 'Private Practice, Public Health', in Friedman, Lester D. (ed.), *British Cinema and Thatcherism: Fires Were Started*, London: UCL Press, 278–293.

Lipton, Lenny (1972) *Independent Filmmaking*, San Francisco: Straight Arrow Books.

LUX (2021) 'About', https://lux.org.uk/about/ (accessed 20 April 2023).

MacDonald, Scott (1998) *A Critical Cinema 3: Interviews with Independent Filmmakers*, Berkeley: University of California Press.

MacDonald, Scott (2006) *A Critical Cinema 5: Interviews with Independent Filmmakers*, Berkeley: University of California Press.

MacDonald, Scott (2016) 'Orpheus of Nitrate: The Emergence of Bill Morrison', *Framework: The Journal of Cinema and Media* 57, no. 2: 116–137.

MacKenzie Scott (2013): ' "An Arrow, Not a Target": Film Process and Processing at the Independent Imaging Retreat', in Hjort, M. (ed.), *The Education of the Filmmaker in Africa, the Middle East, and the Americas,* Global Cinema, New York: Palgrave Macmillan, 169–184.

MacKenzie, Scott & Marchessault, Janine (2019) *Process Cinema: Handmade Film in the Digital Age*, Montreal: McGill-Queen's University Press.

Makino Takashi (n.d.) *Makino Takashi*, https://makinotakashi.net/makinotakashi.html (accessed 13 January 2023).

Malaspina, Cecile (2018) *An Epistemology of Noise*, London: Bloomsbury Academic.

Malone, Micah J. (2021) 'A Conversation with Louise Bourque', in Broomer, Stephen & Enns, Clint (eds.), *Imprints The Films of Louise Bourque*, Ottawa: Canadian Film Institute.

Manovich, Lev (2001) *The Language of New Media*, Cambridge, MA: MIT Press.

Margulis, Lynn (1998) *Symbiotic Planet: A New Look at Evolution*, New York: Basic Books.

Marks, Laura U. (2002) *Touch: Sensuous Theory and Multisensory Media*, Minneapolis: University of Minnesota Press.

May-Simera, Helen, Nagel-Wolfrum, Kerstin & Wolfrum, Uwe (2017) 'Cilia – the Sensory Antennae in the Eye', *Progress in Retinal and Eye Research* 60: 144–180.

McKay, George (ed.) (1998) *DiY Culture: Party and Protest in Nineties Britain*, London: Verso.

Metamkine (n.d.) *Textes*, http://metamkine.free.fr/metamnotes.htm (accessed 26 August 2022).

Moholy-Nagy, László (1947) *Vision in Motion*, Chicago: P. Theobald.

Monk, Claire (2014) ' "*The Shadow of this Time*": Punk, Tradition, and History in Derek Jarman's *Jubilee* (1987)', *Shakespeare Bulletin* 32, no. 3 (Fall): 359–373.

Morgan, Eleanor (2016) *Gossamer Days: Spiders, Humans and Their Threads*, London: Strange Attractor Press.

Morton, Timothy (2007) *Ecology without Nature*, Cambridge, MA: Harvard University Press.

Morton, Timothy (2017) *Humankind: Solidarity with Nonhuman People*, London: Verso.

Michel, Basile & Ambrosino, Charles (2019) 'Territorialised or without Commitment: An In-Depth Analysis of "Cultural and Creative" Activities in a Post-Industrial Neighbourhood in Grenoble', translated from French by Aruna Popuri, *L'Espace Géographique* 48, no. 1: 1–20.

Munkholm, Johan Lau (2018) 'Promises of Uncertainty: A Study of Afrofuturist Interventions into the Archive', *Journal of Science Fiction* 2, no. 2 (January): 47–63.

Murphy, K. & Fox, M. D. (2017) 'Towards a Consensus Regarding Global Signal Regression for Resting State Functional Connectivity MRI', *NeuroImage*, no. 154: 169–173.

Nadolny, Sten (2004) *The Discovery of Slowness*, Edinburgh: Canongate.

Nagel, Thomas (1974) 'What Is It Like to Be a Bat?', *Philosophical Review* 83, no. 4 (October): 435–450.

Navire Argo (2022) 'At the Former Éclair Laboratory', https://navireargo.org/en/at-the-former-eclair-laboratory/ (accessed 14 December 2022).

National Park Service (2020) *Sound Library*, https://www.nps.gov/yell/learn/photosmulti media/soundlibrary.htm (accessed 16 January 2023).

Nieman, Anna (2013) 'Anna Niemans Interview with Pavel Kostomarov and Alexander Rastorguev on their film Я Тебя Люблю (I Love You)', http://giuvivrussianfilm.blogspot.com/2013/03/anna-niemans-interview-with-pavel.html (accessed 12 March 2020).

Nishikawa, Tomonari (2021) 'Film/Video', https://www.tomonarinishikawa.com/film.html (accessed 14 December 2022).

O'Pray, Michael (2009) ' "New Romanticism" and British Avant-Garde Film in the Early 80s', in Murphy, Robert (ed.), *The British Cinema Book,* 3rd ed., London: Palgrave Macmillan & British Film Institute, 343–349.

Pascoe, Bruce (2018) *Dark Emu,* London: Scribe Publications.

Pereira, Michela (2000a) 'Alchemy and Hermeticism: An Introduction to This Issue', *Alchemy and Hermeticism, Early Science and Medicine* 5, no. 2: 115–120.

Pereira, Michela (2000b) 'Heavens on Earth. From the Tabula Smaragdina to the Alchemical Fifth Essence Early Science and Medicine', *Alchemy and Hermeticism* 5, no. 2: 131–144.

Pope, Greg (2011) *Loophole Cinema,* https://gregpope.org/loophole-cinema/ (accessed 7 September 2022).

Raekstad, Paul & Gradin, Sofa Saio (2020): *Prefigurative Politics: Building Tomorrow Today,* Cambridge: Polity.

Ramey, Kathryn (2015) *Experimental Filmmaking: Break the Machine,* New York: Focal.

Read, John (1933) 'Alchemy and Alchemists', *Folklore* 44, no. 3 (September): 251–278.

Re-Engineering the Moving Image (2016) 'About', http://re-mi.mire-exp.org/about (accessed 14 December 2022).

Rekveld, Joost (2006) Film #2, http://www.joostrekveld.net/wp/?p=92 (accessed 26 August 2022).

Rhodes, Christopher J. (2017) 'The Whispering World of Plants: "The Wood Wide Web" ', *Science Progress* 100, no. 3: 331–337.

Rony, Fatimah Toby (2003) 'The Quick and the Dead: Surrealism and the Found Ethnographic Footage Films of Bontoc Eulogy and Mother Dao: The Turtlelike', *Camera Obscura,* 129–155.

Rosales, Jennifer Ann (2013): 'Participatory Culture at the Echo Park Film Center', *Journal of Media Literacy Education* 5, no.1, https://digitalcommons.uri.edu/jmle/vol5/iss1/7 (accessed 26 April 2019).

Rossin, Federico (2007) 'What Remains to Be Seen – Interview with Phil Solomon', *Dérives,* http://derives.tv/what-remains-to-be-seen-interview-with-phil-solomon/ (accessed 12 January 2023).

Roussel, Raymond (2011) *Impression of Africa,* translated by Lindy Foord & Rayner Heppenstall, Richmond: Oneworld Classics.

Sachs, Lynn, Harris, Christopher, Hopinka, Sky, Finley, Jeanne C. & Mohaiemen, Naeem, (2018) 'English Is Spoken Here / English Is Broken Here / A Conversation about Film and Language', *World Records Journal* 2, https://worldrecordsjournal.org/english-is-spoken-here-english-is-broken-here/ (accessed 17 April 2023).

Sagan, Lynn (1967) 'On the Origin of Mitosing Cells', *Journal of Theoretical Biology* 14: 225–274.

Sargeant, Jack (1995) *Deathtripping: The Cinema of Transgression*, London: Creation Books.

Schefer, Raquel (2022) 'Perspectives Dialectically Intersected: The Mexican Audiovisual Collective Los Ingrávidos and Its Film Coyolxauhqui (2017)', *Jump Cut: A Review of Contemporary Media* 61 (Fall), https://www.ejumpcut.org/currentissue/RaquelSchefer/text.html (accessed 17 April 2023).

Shryane, Jennifer (2011) *Blixa Bargeld and Einstürzende Neubauten: German Experimental Music 'Evading do-re-mi'*, Farnham: Ashgate Books.

Sicinski, Michael (2007) 'Phil Solomon Visits San Andreas and Escapes, Not Unscathed', *Cinema Scope* 30: 30–33.

Simard, Suzanne, Perry, David A., Jones, Melanie D., Myrold, David D., Durall, Daniel M. & Molina, Randy (1997) 'Net Transfer of Carbon between Ectomycorrhizal Tree Species in the Field', *Nature* 388: 579–582.

Skinner, Burrhus Rederic (2009) *About Behaviorism*, New York: Random House.

Smith, Vicky (2019) 'Not (a) Part: Handmade Animation, Materialism and the Photogram Film', *International Journal of Creative Media Research*, no. 2 (September).

Smith, Vicky & Hamlyn, Nicky (2018) *Experimental and Expanded Animation: New Perspectives and Practices*, Cham: Palgrave McMillan.

Sobchack, Vivian (2004) *Carnal Thoughts: Embodiment and Moving Image Culture*, Berkeley: University of California Press.

St John, Graham (2014) *Rave Culture and Religion*, Abingdon: Routledge.

Strupele, Inese (2017) 'Latvian Amateur Documentary Film, 1970s–1980s: Family, Community, Travel, and Politics in the Films of Lapiņš, Ingvars Leitis, and Zigurds Vidiņš', *Culture Crossroads* 10, http://www.culturecrossroads.lv/index.php/cc/article/view/142 (accessed 14 December 2022).

Sweeney, Megan & McCouch, Susan (2007) 'The Complex History of the Domestication of Rice', *Annals of Botany* 100, no. 5: 951–957.

Takahashi, Tess (2021) 'Fukushima Abstractions: *Sound of a Million Insects, Light of a Thousand Stars* as Analog Data Visualization', *ASAP/Journal* 6, no. 1 (January): 67–77.

ter Meulen, B. C., Tavy, D. & Jacobs, B. C. (2009) 'From Stroboscope to Dream Machine: A History of Flicker-Induced Hallucinations', *European Neurology* 62, no. 5: 316–320.

Tian, Feng, Stevens, Natalie & Buckler, Edward (2009) 'Tracking Footprints of Maize Domestication and Evidence for a Massive Selective Sweep on Chromosome 10', *Proceedings of the National Academy of Sciences of the United States of America* 106, 9979–9986.

Toop, David (2016) *Into the Maelstrom: Music, Improvisation and the Dream of Freedom*, New York: Bloomsbury.

Tribeca Festival (2020) 'L'Eclat du Mal', https://tribecafilm.com/festival/archive/
512cdaee1c7d76e0460001ca-l-eclat-du-mal (accessed 27 January 2023).

Turner, Mark W. (2009) 'Derek Jarman in the Docklands: The Last of England and Thatcher's
London', in Rhodes, John David & Gorfinkel, Elena (eds.), *Taking Place: Location and the
Moving Image*, Minneapolis: University of Minnesota Press, 77–94.

Urlus, Esther (2013) 'Books', Esther Urlus, https://estherurlus.hotglue.me/d-i-y (accessed
14 December 2022).

van der Zande, Erwin (1994) 'The Young Ones Are Go!' *Blvd.* #8, September, 54–59.

van de Sande, Mathijs (2020) 'They Don't Represent Us? Synecdochal Representation and
the Politics of Occupy Movements', *Constellations* 27: 397–411.

van Houdt, Reinier (n.d.) *Vision*, https://www.reiniervanhoudt.nl/htm/vision.htm
(accessed 16 January 2023).

Vertov, Dziga & Michelson, Annette (2001) *Kino-Eye: The Writings of Dziga Vertov*,
Berkeley: University of California Press.

Vetlesen, Arne Johan (2019) *Cosmologies of the Anthropocene: Panpsychism, Animism, and
the limits of Posthumanism*, London: Routledge.

Viveiros de Castro, Eduardo (2017) *Cannibal Metaphysics*, Minneapolis: University of
Minnesota Press.

Vriens, Jorne (2016) *Het kunstenaarsinitiatief in de jaren tachtig* [Artist-run spaces in
the 1980s], master's thesis, Utrecht University, https://studenttheses.uu.nl/handle/
20.500.12932/22535 (accessed 9 August 2022).

Walley, Jonathan (2020) *Cinema Expanded: Avant-Garde Film in the Age of Intermedia*,
New York: Oxford University Press.

Williams, Scott (1995) A Use for That Last Cup of Coffee: Film and Paper Development,
DCCT (September–October), https://scholarworks.rit.edu/article/1124/ (accessed
13 January 2023).

Wood, David M.J. (2010) 'Film and the Archive: Nation, Heritage, Resistance', *Cosmos and
History: Journal of Natural and Social Philosophy* 6, no. 2 (2010): 162–174.

Wynn-Williams C. G. 2016. *Surveying the Skies: How Astronomers Map the Universe*,
Switzerland: Springer.

Xcèntric (2009) *Paraula D'Autor: Eve Heller, Last Lost, Xcèntric*, http://xcentric.cccb.org/en/
cataleg/fitxa/paraula-dautor-eve-heller-last-lost/225189 (accessed 27 January 2023).

Yong, Ed (2016) *I Contain Multitudes: The Microbes Within Us and a Grander View of Life*,
London: Harper Collins.

Yue, Genevieve (2015) 'Kitchen Sink Cinema: Artist-Run Film Laboratories', *Film Comment*,
https://www.filmcomment.com/blog/artist-run-film-laboratories/ (accessed 26 May, 2023).

Zedd, Nick (1985) 'Cinema of Transgression Manifesto', *Underground Film Bulletin*, New York.

Zinman, Gregory (2014) 'Between Canvas and Celluloid: Painted Films and Filmed Paintings', *Moving Image Review & Art Journal (Miraj)* 3, no. 2: 162–176.

Zinman, Gregory (2020) *Making Images Move: Handmade Cinema and the Other Arts*, Berkeley: University of California Press.

Filmography

#2 – Joost Rekveld (NL 1993, 16mm film, colour, 12min)

Alchemie – Jürgen Reble & Thomas Köner (DE 1992, expanded cinema, 45min), https://filmalchemist.de/performances/alchemie.html

Alone, Life Wastes Andy Hardy – Martin Arnold (AT 1998, 16mm film, bw, 14min)

The Angelic Conversation – Derek Jarman (UK 1984, 35mm film, colour, 77min)

Aus den Algen – Schmelzdahin (DE 1986, Super 8 film, colour, 10min)

Begone Dull Care – Norman McLaren & Evelyn Lambart (CA 1949, 16mm film, colour, 7min)

Berlin, Symphonie einer Großstad – Walter Ruttmann (DE 1927, 35mm film, bw, 64min), https://www.youtube.com/watch?v=TVqPoV9q4ck

Blutrausch – Thorsten Fleisch (DE 1999, 16mm film, colour, 4min), https://vimeo.com/3859031.

Cailloux, Rocher, Algues – David Dudouit (FR 2009, Super 8 film, bw, 5min)

Caravaggio – Derek Jarman (UK 1986, 35mm film, colour, 93min)

Cinema'a o de Cómo Curar el Mal de Archivo – Elena Pardo (MX 2016, HD video, colour, 12min), https://www.elenapardo.com/film

Circus of the Senses – Loophole Cinema (UK 1993, expanded cinema, 60min)

A Colour Box – Len Lye (UK 1935, 16mm film, colour, 3min)

Das Cabinet des Dr. Caligari – Robert Wiene (DE 1920, 35mm film, bw, 74min), https://www.youtube.com/watch?v=7P8jSHFxcrA

Das Goldene Tor – Jürgen Reble (DE 1992, 16mm film, colour, 55min)

Deconstruction Site – Dominic Angerame (US 1990, 16mm film, bw, 12min)

Dervish Machine – Jeanne Liotta & Bradley Eros (US 1992, 16mm film, bw & colour, 10min)

Die Botschaft – Totentanz 8 – Michael Brynntrup (DE 1989, Super 8 film, bw, 10min), https://vimeo.com/353615170

Die Statik der Eselsbrücken – Michael Brynntrup (DE 1990, 16mm film, bw, 20min), https://vimeo.com/137294503

Effects of Darkened Rooms – Loophole Cinema (UK 1990, expanded cinema installation)

...ere erera baleibu izik subua aruaren... – José Antonio Sistiaga (ES 1970, 35mm film, colour, 75min)

The Exiles – Kent Mackenzie (US 1961, 16mm film, bw, 72min), https://archive.org/details/theexiles

Fingered – Richard Kern & Lydia Lunch (US 1986, Super 8 film, bw, 25min)

Fort/Vlees – Karel Doing (NL 1987, Super 8 film, bw, 9min), https://vimeo.com/241028645

Haarlem – Willy Mullens (NL 1922, 35mm film, tinted bw, 7min)

Hondekoppen – Saskia Fransen & Karel Doing (NL 1990, 16mm film, bw, 2min)

I Love You / Я Тебя Люблю – Pavel Kostomarov & Alexander Rastorguev (RU 2011, HD video, colour, 80min), https://www.youtube.com/watch?v=cIUbYIBye90&t=1s

Images of a Moving City – Karel Doing (NL 2001, 35mm film, bw, 37min)

It Matters What – Francisca Duran (CA 2019, HD video, colour & bw, 9min)

Jáaji Approx – Sky Hopinka (US 2015, HD video, colour, 8min), https://vimeo.com/126297131

Jesus – The Film – Michael Bryntrupp (DE 1981, Super 8 film, bw, 125min), https://vimeo.com/115472022

A Journey to Tarakan – Karel Doing (NL 2002, 35mm film, colour & bw, 47min), https://vimeo.com/236095965

Jours en Fleurs – Louise Bourque (CA 2003, 16mm film, colour, 5min)

Konrad & Kurfurst – Esther Urlus (NL 2014, 16mm film, colour, 7min), https://vimeo.com/125262000

Landfill 16 – Jennifer Reeves (US 2011, 16mm film, colour, 9min), https://vimeo.com/35139986

L'Ange – Patrick Bokanowski (FR 1982, 35mm film, colour, 70min)

The Last Angel of History – John Akomfrah (UK 1996, SD video, colour, 45min)

Last Lost – Eve Heller (US 1996, 16mm film, bw, 14min)

The Last of England – Derek Jarman (UK 1987, 35mm film, colour & bw, 87min)

L'Éclat du Mal / The Bleeding Heart of It – Louise Bourque (CA 2005, 16mm film, colour, 6min)

Lichtjaren – Karel Doing (NL 1993, Super 8 film, colour, 7min), https://vimeo.com/236724304

Line Describing a Cone – Anthony McCall (UK 1973, expanded cinema, 30min), https://vimeo.com/29428835

Liquidator – Karel Doing (NL 2010, 35mm film, tinted bw, 8min), https://www.youtube.com/watch?v=36Xise_Nr2s

Looking for Apoekoe – Karel Doing (NL/SR 2010, 16mm film, colour & bw, 13min)

Lyrical Nitrate – Peter Delpeut (NL 1991, 35mm film, tinted bw, 50min), https://vimeo.com/ 523287551

Maas Observation – Greg Pope & Karel Doing (NL 1997, 16mm film, bw, 11min), https:// vimeo.com/92404110

Man with a Movie Camera / Человек с Киноаппаратом – Dziga Vertov (RU 1929, 35mm film, bw, 68min), https://www.youtube.com/watch?v=cGYZ5847FiI

Memento Stella – Takashi Makino (JP 2018, 4K video, colour, 60min)

Meni – Karel Doing (NL 1992, Super 8 film, bw, 3min), https://vimeo.com/64876323

Mijkrēšļa rotaļa ar spoguli / Twilight Play with a Mirror – Ivars Skanstiņš (LV 1972, 16mm film, bw, 15min)

Mother Dao, the Turtlelike – Vincent Monnikendam (NL 1995, 35mm film, bw, 90min)

The Mulch Spider's Dream – Karel Doing (UK 2018, 16mm film, colour, 14min), https:// vimeo.com/286533221

Nervous System – Ken Jacobs (US 1975–2000, expanded cinema, variable length)

Noisy Licking, Dribbling and Spitting – Vicky Smith (UK 2014, 16mm film, colour, 4min), https://vimeo.com/134938105

Not (a) Part – Vicky Smith (UK 2019, 16mm film, bw, 6min), https://vimeo.com/429337626

Oxygen – Karel Doing (UK 2023, 16mm film, colour, 6min)

Passage a l'Acte – Martin Arnold (AT 1993, 16mm film, bw, 12min)

A Perfect Storm – Karel Doing (UK 2022, 16mm film, colour, 3min)

Phytography – Karel Doing (UK 2020, 16mm film, colour, 8min)

Pièce Touchée – Martin Arnold (AT 1989, 16mm film, bw, 16min)

Premonition – Dominic Angerame (US 1995, 16mm film, bw, 10min)

Primal – Vicky Smith (UK 2017, 16mm film, colour, 9min), https://vimeo.com/188411688

Propaganda Beacons – Loophole Cinema (UK 1991, expanded cinema installation)

Recollection – Pierre Bastien & Karel Doing (NL 1998, expanded cinema, colour & bw, 45min)

Regen – Joris Ivens (NL 1929, 35mm film, bw, 14min), https://vimeo.com/120679815

Remains to Be Seen – Phil Solomon (CA 1989, 16mm film, colour, 17min)

The Right Side of My Brain – Lydia Lunch & Henry Rollins (US 1985, Super 8 film, bw, 23min)

Riuh Saudara / Vociferous Family – Etienne Caire, Joyce Lainé & Loïc Verdillon (FR/ID/AU 2018, expanded cinema, colour, 25min)

Rotary Factory – Pierre Bastien & Karel Doing (NL 1996, expanded cinema, bw, 30min), https://vimeo.com/92382983

Saamaka – Karel Doing (NL/SR 2010, SD video, bw, 50min)

Schwechater – Peter Kubelka (AT 1958, 16mm film, bw, 1min)

Shadow Engine – Loophole Cinema (UK 1991, expanded cinema, 40min)

Skin Film 2 – Emma Hart (UK 20052007, 16mm film, colour, 11min), https://vimeo.com/37338288

Small Things Moving in Unison – Vicky Smith (UK 2018, 16mm film, bw, 5min), https://vimeo.com/300496214

Sound of a Million Insects, Light of a Thousand Stars – Tomonari Nishikawa (US 2014, 16mm film, colour, 2min), https://vimeo.com/117525500

The Sound We See: A Los Angeles City Symphony – Echo Park Film Center (US 2010, 16mm film, bw, 27min), https://vimeo.com/92652595

Submit to Me – Richard Kern (US 1986, Super 8 film, colour, 12min), https://vimeo.com/59420147

The Sun Quartet – Colectivo Los Ingrávidos (MX 2017, 16mm film, colour, 61min), https://vimeo.com/203563626

Tabula Smaragdina – Jürgen Reble (DE 1997, expanded cinema, colour, 45min)

Vacant Procession – Loophole Cinema (UK 1993, expanded cinema)

Variations on a Cellophane Wrapper – David Rimmer (CA 1972, 16mm film, colour, 8min), https://vimeo.com/125224440

Vitaal Filmen – Rob Sweere, Ania Rachmat, Kana Miloning, Saskia Fransen, Edward Luyken, Jaap Kroneman, Job Horst, Ida Lohman/Fiona Tan, Doro Krol, Karel Doing & Luk Sponselee (NL 1993, Super 8 film, colour & bw, 32min), https://lightcone.org/fr/film-1396-vitaal-filmen

Vlaag – Karel Doing (NL 1988, Super 8 film, bw, 1min)

Weltenempfanger – Schmelzdahin (DE 1985, Super 8 film, colour, 5min)

When It Was Blue – Jennifer Reeves (US 2008, 16mm film, colour, 68min)

Whirlwind – Loophole Cinema & Karel Doing (NL/UK 1998, 16mm film, colour, 9min), https://vimeo.com/64874708

Wilderness Series – Karel Doing (UK 2016, 2K video, colour, 13min), https://vimeo.com/243624614

Wolkenschatten – Anja Dornieden & David Monroy Gonzalez (DE 2014, 16mm film, colour, 17min)

The World – Takashi Makino (JP 2009, 16mm film, bw, 51min)

Index